SALES COP'

M000012868

ADVANCED PUBLISHING AND MARKETING STRATEGIES FOR INDIE AUTHORS

SELF-PUBLISHING GUIDE BOOK FOUR

Robert J. Ryan

Cover design by 187designz

ISBN: 9781711904504
(print edition)

Trotting Fox Press

Contents

Introduction

Words are the tools of choice for authors. Words are their passion and their craft. But true sales copy is as different from normal writing as English is from another language.

Could you write a masterpiece in a language you don't speak?

Not an easy task! But just like any foreign language, sales copy has its own grammar and vocabulary. It has learnable principles of what works and what doesn't. Do you want to unlock them and turn them to your benefit?

I think you do. Otherwise, you wouldn't be reading this.

Can I ask you some questions?

Do you know what *truly* persuades a reader to open an email after reading the subject line? Have you doubled the subscription rate to your author newsletter by breaking away from standard advice on how to request signups? Have you been taught that your author biography is a sales tool similar to a blurb?

I'm guessing the answer is no to the first two questions. And I suspect you've never even heard anyone talk about how to do the last.

Welcome to professional-level sales copy. It'll change your world, and the goal of this book is to teach it to you.

Every word you publish is a point of contact with readers. Every word you write is a word that will persuade people to keep reading, and maybe buy, or to stop reading and never buy. Whatever you write, and wherever it appears, is an opportunity to persuade.

Or a lost opportunity…

This book will teach you how to seize opportunities you never saw before. And having seized what others who follow standard advice miss, it'll show you how to persuade.

Not for a bad purpose. Not to *sell* something to somebody. That's low-level marketing. High-level sales copy doesn't try to sell something. It connects a buyer to a product they *want*. It keeps them reading while they make that decision.

Sales copy is an art. Like fiction. But it's a science too. It draws heavily on neuroscience. Where the two intersect is called neuromarketing.

In the old days, everything was done by instinct and trial and error. Now, research verifies much of what the old copywriting masters knew, and it suggests new possibilities.

This book brings both approaches together, and applies it specifically to the everyday publishing tasks of authors, fiction and nonfiction alike. Amazon sellers, bloggers and anyone with an interest in marketing or persuasion will benefit too.

Sales copy comes in many forms. Sometimes it's called copywriting. It's used by amateurs and professionals alike, but at heart, whatever it's called and whatever its specific purpose, it has one main goal: to persuade.

So then, who am I to give advice on the art and science of persuasion?

Before I quit my job in March 2018 to become a full-time author, I worked for the government. Try not to hold a grudge against me. What I did there revolved around ensuring people complied with legislative requirements.

Worse, they were *tax* requirements.

Still holding that grudge at bay?

My core task was ensuring people complied with legislation … and often people would rather *not*. This is a problem all governments face, and not just for tax. As a result, they employ teams of people with copywriting, behavioral economics, behavioral insight and marketing skillsets. Their brief? Persuade people to do the right thing. Or at least what the legislation says is the right thing…

I was one of them. I was a persuader.

You might be surprised how seriously some government departments take this. My department took it so seriously that we had access to regular focus groups, a support network across interstate and multijurisdictional lines and novelties like infrared eye-tracking technology. This technology allows research into how people read a web page, how they read a letter and what they look at and don't look at. We used every tool at our disposal to monitor what worked, and what didn't.

That's what I did. And I specialized in copywriting techniques. Others I worked with included behavioral psychologists, qualitative market research scientists and behavioral economists. We learned off each other and pooled our skills together to get the job done.

My work covered a wide field. Letters. Websites. Strategic advice on communication methods. Drafting ads for industry journals. Advising on training methods. Providing lectures to staff on the basic principles of copywriting. Heading a video project and drafting the script for it. Interesting stuff (but not as much fun as writing fiction).

That's who I was.

Now, I'm a fulltime author. My fiction is published under a pen name as well as my real name – Robert Ryan. For nonfiction, I insert a J.

And what have I achieved as an indie author? Long story short: freedom. I work for myself. I'm my own boss, and I earn a comfortable living. Comfortable enough that part of my writing schedule involves a post-lunch nana nap. Something that my copywriting skills never convinced a government boss to approve. Go figure.

Now, your goals may not be the same as mine. If not, I urge you to at least consider the nana nap. But whatever they are, I'm pretty sure they involve finding ways to take your writing craft and infuse it with publishing expertise and marketing savvy so you can break out and reach the next level.

It can be done. I've done it. Sales copy is a critical factor in the process. In short, I know what you want to know, and the rest of this book provides that knowledge.

1. What Good Sales Copy Can Do

Words matter.

Words can change the world. Words *have* changed the world.

Words matter, because they persuade people. And they do it with emotion.

Sure, you can fill copy with facts, figures, benefits and reasons why someone should do something. To some extent, you should.

But it doesn't work well by itself. Emotion persuades people. Facts trigger disputes.

This is because my "fact" may not be your "fact".

Marketing has been around a long time. In the digital age, it's exploded to saturation point. It's inescapable, with the average person bombarded by about 5,000 ads a day. For this reason, much of the old model of advertising doesn't work so well anymore. People increasingly resist it, because they recognize it for what it is. Manipulation. The term for this is psychological reactance, and it can kill your sales copy. Dead.

Buy now!
Wait, there's more!
You'll never believe…
Grab your copy today!

All old school. All less effective than they used to be.

This poses a question. What *is* effective?

The answer is what's always been effective, and what's persuaded people since the origin of humanity. It's what will remain effective even in a future world where the human mind taps wirelessly into the internet to download data direct to the brain.

Emotion.

Emotion, expressed through words, has changed (and will always change) the world.

I have a dream…
…we shall never surrender…
Mr. Gorbachev. Tear down this wall!
We choose to go to the moon.

Grab your copy today! It doesn't seem persuasive now, does it?

And yet marketing has learned. It's catching up to the digital age. Neuroscience is at the cutting edge of this. Not only does it confirm what we already know is persuasive, it tells us why.

Let's delve into that briefly.

To do so, we'll look at one of the modern world's best bits of sales copy. This happens to be a slogan, but whole campaigns have been built around it.

JUST DO IT.

That, of course, is the Nike slogan.

Is it giving you information? Is it selling benefits? Is it appealing to you intellectually? Is it making an argument for why Nike products are better, and you should buy them?

No. Its tapping into a deeper level of the human psyche. The yearning to achieve. The desire to fulfil your goals. The will to become the best you can be. If it were music, it would be the *Rocky* theme.

The slogan makes no logical arguments, but fires up your emotions.

How well did it perform as a slogan? It allowed Nike over a ten-year period (1988 to 1998) to increase sport-shoe sales in North America from 877 million to 9.2 *billion*.

That's success on a stupendous scale.

And that's what sales copy can do. To be sure, there would have been a lot of other things going on at Nike as well. Ad spend must have helped too!

But *why* does emotion work to sell?

This is the neuroscience. Emotions are powerful. They tell us what to do. If one of our ancestors saw a nice, ripe juicy fruit hanging from a tree, the positive emotional response was anticipation of pleasure. *Yummy yummy, get in my tummy*. Or something like that.

On the other hand, if our ancestors saw a sabre-tooth tiger on the prowl, the negative emotional response was fear. *Eek! Run, Forrest, run!*

Emotions keep us alive. They make our lives better, and safer. We don't even need to think about them. They just *are*. They well up from deep inside us and take control.

You may be interested that the amygdalae are the parts of the brain chiefly responsible. They're set deep within the more primitive areas, one in the left hemisphere and one in the right. And just like the left side of the brain is different from the right, so too is each amygdala. The left one is associated with rewards and positive emotions, the right with negative emotions.

What's important for us to understand right now is that these clusters of neurons play a primary role in emotional responses. And decision making. It's also believed they play a role in the brain's reward system, but we'll explore how sales copy uses that in later chapters.

For now, this is what's important. Certain emotions trigger a release of dopamine. Dopamine isn't just the "feel good" chemical. It also stimulates us to take action to move toward rewarding situations. So, positive emotions give us a feel-good hit and excite us to act.

Think about that, and what it means for how you word your sales copy.

Think about that in terms of the Nike slogan.

It's also interesting that the Nike logo (artfully called the Swoosh) is actually a tick. A tick is a symbol for good things and associated with positive emotions. As an aside, Amazon's logo with the curved arrow under their name suggests a smiley face.

Coincidence? Evidence that multibillion-dollar companies place great importance on emotional marketing?

You decide.

Higher parts of the brain, the parts involved with strategic planning and problem solving, can override emotions.

But often they don't. More likely, if you *feel* that something is good or bad you just act accordingly. And if you do rationalize, you'll come up with logical reasons to support your emotional response, not to contradict it.

In truth, our emotions are often a better basis for decisions than rational thought. This is because, historically, emotions kept us alive. Their purpose in fact, is to keep us alive and ensure we reproduce and raise offspring.

All this is making a point.

Emotions are critical to people. They get our attention and focus it faster, and stronger, than anything else. Just like the fetid breath and flashing teeth of a sabre-tooth tiger would get more of your attention than an engineering analysis of the pound per square inch force capable of being exerted by said teeth.

Emotions get our attention. This is also the first aim of sales copy. Get attention. No eyeballs on your copy means no sales.

Interesting, yes?

But wait, there's more. (Seems those words aren't quite outdated after all.)

When we're flushed with positive emotion, we tend to reach out for something good (the fruit). When we have no emotion, we have no real drive to act. When we have a bad emotion (fear of a sabre-tooth tiger) our action tends to be running away.

Translating these ancient instincts into the modern digital world means that if you engage someone emotionally first, you'll get their attention and they'll be more likely to act on what you're saying.

But be careful.

The positive emotion and your end goal should match. The moment you try to manipulate someone into doing something not good for them (e.g. trying to convince them to buy something they don't really want) is the moment you risk starting up what neuroscience and psychology call reactance. It's the mind's self-defense mechanism. It drives the person to want to do the exact *opposite* of what you want.

This is why good marketing always tries to connect a person to a product that they actually want.

There you have it. It's interesting stuff, even if it's just a brief explanation of what sales copy can do, and how emotion works in advertising. But there's much, much more for neuroscience to tell us.

For instance, how do hooks work, and how can we make them better?

We'll touch again and again on neuroscience as this book continues. It links with sales copy in so many ways, and offers meaning to why many old ideas actually work and ways to make copywriting more effective in the future.

This isn't a science textbook though, so while I'll mention neuroscience wherever it sheds light on a topic, I promise not to get too geeky on you.

So, to summarize. Use emotion in your copy. It gets attention, and it's more effective than trying to convince someone why they should do something.

2. Reactance Kills Sales

Have you ever herded cattle?

Herding cattle is an art. If you've done it, and done it the wrong way (as I have), the ornery critters will go anywhere and everywhere but where you want them to.

Why should that be?

The cattle know they're being manipulated. They don't like it. They have an instinct to resist, because in the wild predators like wolves try to herd them so they can separate the weakest out of the herd and set it up for a kill. Sometimes, a few members of the pack drive an animal toward an ambush by other packmates.

People share similar instincts to cattle. The more you try to convince someone to do something, the more they choose to do the opposite. They know you want something, likely money, and they resist. This is why overt marketing is ineffective.

Neuroscientists, as we've discovered, call this reactance.

What types of copy trigger reactance?

Anything that tries to take away someone's freedom of choice. Freedom of choice is a fundamental human right. It's fundamental, because it's based on psychological instinct just like it is with the cattle.

Wolves may not stalk and herd people, but poor advertising tries to do the same thing with words. And the moment people realize that they're being herded, reactance forms.

There's a conundrum here. Copywriters know that a good call to action (CTA) works. And good CTAs usually come in the form of a command. For instance, buy now.

Shouldn't this cause reactance?

What's happening here is that the CTA comes right at the end of the sales funnel. Everything that's come before it will either have persuaded the prospective buyer (prospect) to buy. Or aroused reactance.

If reactance is going on, a command CTA isn't going to work. Probably nothing is going to work. You've had your chance in the sales copy, and blown it.

But if the copy was persuasive, then the prospect has buying intent. The buy CTA actually resonates with what they already want to do, and in the digital world at least the CTA is both a command and the actual means to buy. It'll usually be a nice blue button. Or a nice blue hyperlink. So it serves as a command, but also as a signal saying "hey, you've decided to buy? This is the place you need to click."

A lot depends on context though. In an environment where buy CTAs are the norm, the command aspect becomes near-invisible. It may have a subtle effect, but it blends in with everything around it in the same way that you don't notice you're breathing all day long. It's there. It's happening. But your mind doesn't focus on it.

What *will* bring a prospect's mind to focus on a command CTA is using it in a place that the prospect isn't accustomed to seeing it. For instance, at the end of a book blurb.

By tradition, a book blurb finishes with a cliffhanger story question. Slipping some sort of buy CTA into that arouses focus (and reactance) like a wolf howling just behind you. And not of the Team Jacob kind. (Team Edward was always my preference anyway. Vampires are *way* cooler than werewolves.)

The moral of the story is this. Know your audience. Speak to them on their terms. They're in charge, not you. Don't try to convince them. Rather, let them make their own choices. Lead them forward by all means, like Gandalf leading the Fellowship of the Ring, but never push them from behind. That's how Saruman would have done it.

I'll let up on the fantasy references, and mosey on back to cattle.

Do you know the easiest way to get a herd into a set of yards or through a gate? Don't try to push them from behind. Stand in front of them and shake a feed bucket. That usually brings them in. Running.

This is because the feed bucket contains something they want. That's feed. Usually grain or molasses.

Sound familiar? In the same way, good marketing connects a prospect to a product they *want*.

Very closely related to all this is the concept of native advertising.

Native advertising doesn't stand out. It's not overt. It doesn't try to convince or talk someone into something. It's natural and flowing and organic to wherever it appears.

In terms of actual ads, it works like this. The Sponsored Product Carousel on an Amazon product page looks, functions and occupies the near-identical space that the organic also-bought carousel does. Essentially, to an unwary eye, it could be taken for the also-bought carousel itself. It has the appearance of being "native".

Estimates vary, but native advertising can perform anywhere up to 50% better than "foreign" advertising.

On an Amazon product page, a Product Display ad, set apart by itself on the right-hand side, is immediately apparent as an ad. For this reason, prospects automatically view it with suspicion. It's an ad, and by its nature it's not to be trusted.

Don't take my word for these things. Google them. Something like "benefits of native advertising" will do the trick.

Of course, the examples given above are actual ads. A refinement of the concept is persuasive copy in, say, backmatter. This might be intended to encourage read-through to the next book in the series.

This type of backmatter advertising will perform better if it's "native" rather than an overt attempt to talk someone into doing something.

Another example of this approach is seen in movies and TV shows. For instance, a reality cooking show where the contestants have to prepare a dish and the camera pans over the ingredients showing the label of a particular brand of milk or something. It's there. It's effectively a paid-for ad. But it's unobtrusive. It's not telling anyone to buy it, but by its (seemingly) organic presence, it doesn't trigger reactance.

Something that made huge news fairly recently was the Starbucks coffee cup left inadvertently in a scene of *Game of Thrones*. But was it really inadvertent? Or was it paid advertising?

You decide.

What matters is that the natural and the organic is more persuasive. The manipulative, and the attempt to reduce prospect choice, triggers reactance.

Keep this principal in mind no matter what type of sales copy you write. No matter that it's a blog article, introduction to a book, backmatter in a book or a Facebook post. Provide genuine value and lead the prospect toward an idea. Then leave them to decide. Leave them with freedom of choice. They have it anyway. Bad copy tries to pretend they don't. Good copy embraces it, and even reminds them of it.

The neuroscience behind that last statement is fascinating. We'll get to it soon. But first, it's time to discuss the two most useful copywriting formulas ever invented. They'll serve you well in innumerable situations. Especially if you phrase things naturally to the context of where the copy appears, and you avoid provoking reactance.

3. The Formulas of Success

There are many formulas used in sales copy by professional copywriters. Here are, I think, the two best. Especially for the types of copy that authors write.

First, AIDA. This stands for attention, interest, desire and action. It aligns with the psychological state of a buyer as they progress through the sales funnel. This is why it works so well.

The sales funnel is a well-defined and documented process that prospects go through before they buy or make another decision such as whether or not to subscribe.

Without eyeballs on the copy, it's impossible for it to do its job. Hence, the formula starts with attention. This draws the eyeballs.

The interest and desire phases telescope together. They form an evaluation stage. The prospect, having had their attention focused, now begins to weigh up the merits of what the copy is saying. This is the danger zone for reactance. The prospect has time here to perceive manipulation if it exists. This is also where most people stop reading or switch off, having decided that there's nothing in it for them to do whatever the copy is asking.

On the other hand, if the copy is good, this is a transformative stage. Interest grows and becomes desire. The prospect sees that there is, in fact, something in this for them.

If so, they move to the final stage. This might be buy, or subscribe, or leave a review or any number of things that author may be trying to achieve. This is the action phase, and it's the culmination of the copy itself. Everything is leading to this point.

That was AIDA. It's an indispensable formula if you're interested in writing effective sales copy. I suggest you Google it and learn more. I recommend you study ads wherever you see them (it doesn't matter if it's on TV, in a magazine or a Sponsored Product carousel on Amazon) and look for that formula at work. Study it. Break it down. Get to know it. This will pay you back a thousandfold.

AIDA is brilliant. But as I said above, there are other formulas. Many are just variations of it though. One that isn't is also just as good in its way. It's used on a mass scale, and I suggest you research it as well. It's especially good for many of the situations an author finds themselves in. The formula goes like this:

Identify the problem
Agitate the problem
Provide the solution

Its approach and appearance are totally different to AIDA, but at heart, if you look closely, you'll see that just like AIDA it aligns with the sales funnel.

The weakness of this formula is in attracting attention. It contains no prompt to do that. But in practice, good copywriters overlay the identify part with an attention device.

How does the formula work?

The prospect may already be aware of a problem they face, or they may not know until you point it out to them. Either way, if it's a genuine problem, they'll then want the solution. At least, if you've targeted properly.

The problem you identify must resonate with your target audience. Athlete's foot is a problem for some people, but if your target prospect doesn't suffer this unsavory malady, what do they care for the solution?

This also shows how the formula works. It's a hook, of a type that marketers call an open loop. But that loop is never closed. Not in the copy. It drives the reader forward through the copy, but when they reach the end – the provide the solution part – the copy will explicitly state that a solution exists, but will require an action to obtain it. For instance, buying a book.

This is not a switch and bait tactic. The solution must be genuine and real. It must lie on the other end of whatever action you want the prospect to take. Failure to deliver that is a mistake of monumental proportions. You'll never be trusted by that person again, and who could blame them?

This formula is particularly good for nonfiction book blurbs. It also works in backmatter and several other places. As we progress through specific types of sales copy, you'll see it at work.

The middle part of the formula, which is to agitate the problem, corresponds to the interest and desire phase of AIDA. By agitating the problem you allow it to register properly on the prospect's mind. It gathers importance and momentum.

So far, so good. You'll meet each of these formulas again and again in the chapters to come. But it's time to turn from theory to actual practice. What follows gives you examples of how to use sales theory in a wide range of applications.

4. Frontmatter Tips and Tricks

The frontmatter of a book is a critical stage in the purchase funnel, but often overlooked. Even by people who claim to be experts in copywriting.

Why that should be, you'll have to ask them. But when you read what follows, go back to some of the industry gurus who claim copywriting expertise and see how well, or even if, they apply these basic copywriting principles.

Before we get into the specifics, let me say this. First impressions count. I've discussed the halo effect in detail in the previous books of this series. I'm not going to go over that ground again. If you haven't read them, Google the term. You're in for an eye-opener. The halo effect is vitally important to writing sales copy and establishing a career as an author. In essence, make the beginning count. Don't let opportunities slip you by. Use every word to create that right first impression. Delete every word that doesn't have to be there.

Or look at it like this. Imagine the entry to a supposedly fabulous restaurant is positioned at the end of a back alley, filled with stinky garbage and bold rats that looked like they wanted to mug you. And were big enough to pull it off.

Would you go inside, or turn around? If you did go inside, would the experience color your appreciation of the food, no matter that it was world class? It would color mine.

Likewise, imagine you walked through a beautiful building to get to that restaurant. Picture marble floors and decorated wall panels. Imagine violinists at its entrance and a polished-oak door with a golden doorknob. That would be a far more inviting experience, and it would color your appreciation of the meal to follow. At least, on average, scientific experiments show that initial perceptions do exactly that for most people, most of the time.

Let's tackle some specifics.

Table of contents

This is a great opportunity for sales copy, but it's missed by many people – including insta-experts who claim to be gurus on sales copy ... in their books on sales copy. Go figure.

Any nonfiction book is intended to solve a problem or provide information on specific subjects. The prospect will likely have read the blurb before they get to the first pages of the book, so they know what the book claims to provide. By looking inside, they're trying to evaluate how accurate those claims are.

A table of contents that runs for a whole page or two like this...

Chapter 1
Chapter 2
Chapter 3

...and on into mind-numbing oblivion is useless. It tells the prospect *nothing*.

This isn't some sort of hook. It's not being mysterious. It's a missed opportunity.

What the chapter titles should do is act as hooks. Each and every one of them should offer insight into the problems the book will solve. Each chapter title should pique interest and heighten prospect curiosity just like the hooks in the blurb. Or the hooks in a blurb tagline. Or the hooks in the subject line of a marketing email.

Here are some sample chapter titles from book one in this series, *Author Unleashed*:

How Pro Marketers Structure Blurbs
Seven Blurb Myths that Kill Sales
Why Great Books Fail
What Amazon Ads do that Other Ads Can't

In a nonfiction book, the chapter titles are a *massive* lever to drive sales. Make them as hooky as possible, just be sure not to turn them into clickbait. That is, make sure you deliver the goods in the book.

What about fiction?

Fiction is harder. But not impossible. The problem is the same if you don't use chapter titles. It's a long boring list of numbers.

You could argue that prospects just skip this part and scroll down to where the real text starts. Or Amazon's preview likely starts at the beginning of chapter one anyway. All valid points, at least for fiction. But even so, the first chapter title in the preview sits in the same place as a tagline in a blurb. It draws the eye. I advise you to use it and write something hooky that signals genre just as you would for a blurb tagline. It does no harm. It likely does you good.

For fiction, you have a choice. For nonfiction, not using hooky chapter names is a rookie error.

Links away from your book

This is fairly common practice, albeit for different reasons.

The link may be to the cover artist's website. Or other books you've written. Perhaps it asks for a review. Or maybe it offers a free book at your website, or maybe it asks the prospect to click to join your mailing list.

I've seen all these things at the front of a book. Here's my opinion of them.

By all means, credit your cover artist. I believe in that. It's not a legal requirement, but it's a common courtesy. I always do it, but I never make it a clickable link. This is because your goal is to sell your book, not advertise someone else's business.

If the prospect clicks away from the Amazon page, they may never come back to buy your book. For them to be looking at your preview on Amazon, you're as close as you can get to a sale. There's nothing to be gained by risking that. There's nothing to be gained by interrupting the process. Now is the time to be pulling the prospect deeper, not inviting them to leave.

I often see people link to other books they've written. At least this is keeping the prospect "in house" so to speak. It can look impressive, if you have a large backlist. But what's to be gained from it?

Sure, they may end up buying another book by you instead of the one they clicked on. But it's a fundamental concept in marketing that the more choices you give prospects, the more uncertain they become. And uncertainty over what to do decreases sales.

In short, there's nothing to be gained and potentially a lot to lose. I don't advise this tactic. The prospect just read the blurb for the book they've now clicked into. Don't put obstacles in their path. Draw them forward.

As for asking for reviews at the front of a book, it's hard to see the logic of this one. Proponents claim it increases their review rate. I'm not about to argue with them. They know their figures, although reviews are so hard to get, and so far and few in between, that it's hard to see how they get enough of a before and after comparison for statistically relevant data.

No matter. In my view, this does more harm than good. My reaction on reading such a request at the beginning of a book that I haven't even purchased (and may never purchase) is this: *Hold on there, buddy. Let's not get carried away. You already want something from me, and you haven't given me anything yet. Are you for real?*

This is not a promising start to the reader and writer relationship. It undermines the halo effect. I should mention at this point that the halo effect has a twin sister. She's called the horns effect. As in devil's horns. But she works the same way in that a bad first impression colors everything that comes after. This will include the decision to buy or not buy.

I suggest you Google "horns effect". Or you can just imagine the opposite of the halo effect. Or maybe Mary Poppins gone wild.

Technically, I made a mistake above. I said what *my* reaction is to a review request at the beginning of a book. In sales copy, you want to try to avoid transposing your own likes and dislikes onto the prospect. But in this case, I'm confident that a lot of people feel the same way. I'll risk it.

Still thinking about Mary Poppins gone wild? Me too. But it's time to move on. Let's discuss linking away from the book preview to your website.

This might just be a link to the website, or it might involve a request to sign up to a mailing list there, or, as often as not, the promise of a free book for going to the website and signing up.

In my view, linking to the website is a mistake. It takes them away from your sales funnel at the front of the book. They may never come back.

I do see the value of the next idea though. Everyone wants more readers on their subscription list. This is gold for the author, but you always have to ask this: what's in it for them? If you want someone to do something, response rates skyrocket when you give them a good reason. And boy, you'll need a good reason to collect someone's email address these days. People hate spam, and giving out email addresses is a surefire way to encourage it. It's easier to wrangle a cellphone out of a teenage girl's hand while she's texting (not that I've tried that) than to get an email address.

This leads to the giveaway of a free book tactic. I don't doubt this works. You're offering the prospect value there. There *is* something in it for them. This is a concept we'll explore in different contexts throughout this book. WIIFM: What's in it for me? This is what prospects want to know, and the better you can answer that the better your sales copy will be.

Personally, I don't do free. So, this is a tactic that I haven't tried. But I've seen the offer of a free book in order to induce a signup to a mailing list quite often. I don't doubt it works. Less commonly it's used at the start of a book, but that's common enough too.

Is it a good idea?

I'm not going to get into the pros and cons of free itself. You'll have already made your choice on that, and it's not my place to try to convince you one way or the other.

The question you have to ask yourself is what is your highest priority? Is it to sell the book a prospect has just clicked on? Or is it to build your subscriber list?

In this specific situation, you can't do both at the same time. If the prospect clicks away to get a free book, they're going to read that first before they do anything else. That could take days or weeks.

On the one hand, you've lost a potential sale. On the other, you've gained a subscriber. Actually, you'll probably gain a lot of subscribers.

I'd expect a buy to take up the free book offer to have a ratio of something like 1:10, or maybe even much higher. Your offer of a free book gets *heaps* more exposure in the frontmatter than the backmatter. Especially if you're promoting the book.

This is a method that will help build your list *fast*. That's a distinct advantage. When you have a new release, your list will be bigger and more effective and generate greater sales and gain better momentum in the store.

On the downside, a list built on free downloads is not as effective as a list built of people who have paid for your books.

Maybe there's a better way of looking at that.

For a free book, the subscriber gives you their email first. Then they read your book, which they may or may not like. For a bought book, where they subscribe via your backmatter, you can be sure they actually like it. Otherwise you were no chance of getting that email address.

As I say, I don't do free, so I'm not in a position to advise which method is best here. If you do offer free, I suggest trialing the offer in the frontmatter of your books and monitoring to see what decrease in paid sales you might have and what increase in subscriber rates you get.

When you have this data, then you're in a position to decide which method you prefer.

If you're considering putting a request to join your mailing list in the frontmatter, and you're not offering some sort of inducement for the prospect, I refer you back to WIIFM.

And the horns effect. Or if you prefer the imagery, Mary Poppins gone wild. But not in a nice way.

These are common. They have the advantage of being short, but unless there's something in it for the prospect, it's clutter that will trigger the horns effect.

Or is it?

You know my motto in this series. Dig deeper.

Generally, it's clutter. Your Aunt Betsy may be important to you, but you can't expect the prospect to share your feelings.

However, it comes down to execution. Here are two examples.

I dedicate this book to Aunt Betsy.

For Aunt Betsy. You taught me to love stories, and I miss you every time I open a book.

The first is bland. The second invokes emotion, and a prospect induced to feel emotion ... well, we covered how effective that was in chapter one.

The second example is doing more though. It makes the author likeable. This is triggering the halo effect. And although it's a dedication, and has nothing to do with the author's writing ability, it does throw a favorable light on it. Subconsciously, the prospect will form an opinion that someone who "loves stories" is a good writer.

Introduction or foreword

Now, we're getting into some serious copywriting. Introductions are longer. They therefore have more potential to sell books, if written with craft. Or, more potential to lose sales if your craft isn't so good.

Introductions and forewords aren't common in fiction. They're very common in nonfiction, though.

I'm not going to quote someone else's introduction for copyright reasons. So here's one I prepared earlier myself. It's from *Author Unleashed*. Quoting this also has the advantage that I don't have to guess or figure out what copywriting tactics the author was using. I *know*.

The introduction is in normal text, and my comments are interspersed in italics.

This is the truth.

An open loop. What is *this supposed truth? Also a bold claim that instigates a reaction in the prospect. Something along the lines of "This better be good, or I'm outta here." All this serves to engage the prospect. They start thinking about what might be ahead, and whether or not they'll agree with it. This pulls them forward to find out.*

Amazon's Kindle Store is massive. It already contains millions of titles, and thousands of new books are added daily – perhaps hourly. Many of them are good. They all fight for their light under the sun, and competition is brutal. Added to that, Amazon is increasingly a pay-to-play platform.

What's described here is a factual representation of today's self-publishing market, which I don't think many people would dispute. My opening sentence wasn't a clickbait type lead, and my copy is starting to prove itself. Trust is increasing. Slowly.

Additionally, I've identified *several major problems that all indie authors struggle with. And I've invested the facts with emotion by phrases such as "They all fight for their light under the sun..." and words like "brutal".*

Fighting for visibility in those conditions is like Bambi shaping up to Godzilla. Godzilla on steroids.

This draws all the problems together under a single banner: the difficulty of obtaining visibility. It pinpoints the problem with a narrow focus, and does so with what I hope passes for humor. Just maybe this book will prove an interesting read as well as educational. Maybe. Humor, by the way, can also be considered an emotion. And, just like other emotions and rewards, is intricately linked to the amygdala.

Interestingly, while humor may or may not be an emotion (I'm not sure anyone really knows) it does instigate a rise in dopamine just like positive emotions do.

But this is another truth. It's less well known, but grasp it and it'll give you strength.

Another open loop. Okay. Where's this going? It also acknowledges that there are different ways of looking at things. Therefore, it doesn't sound like the author is intent on herding prospects toward some supposed one great truth. Also, the "less well known" part is doing what copywriters call "creating scarcity". A sense of scarcity is rocket fuel to sales. I suggest you Google something like "creating scarcity marketing" for verification and research.

Despite the difficulties, people succeed. Many of them are veterans of indie publishing. But quite a lot are new.

This keeps the open loop going, and intensifies it. That new authors can, and do, succeed is a twist. What is this other truth?

Whatever it is though, it offers hope. Perhaps there's a solution to these problems.

There are ways to rise from under the shadow of competition, and to feel the sun on your face. There are ways to make a full-time living at this business. Every day, people quit their jobs to do so.

Yarg! Enough already. This is more than hope. This is the promise of a downright solution to the visibility problem. But what *is it?*

The last few paragraphs have also been agitating the problem. And simultaneously, generating emotion. Writing as a full-time author is the dream. So is quitting a humdrum job the prospect likely hates.

What do they know? What are their skillsets? How is it they do what others can't?

For the love of all things holy, just tell me!

There are answers to those questions. I've learned a few of them. I continue to learn more. At any rate, I had learned enough by March 2, 2018, to quit my job. I've been a full-time author since then, and I wish I'd done it sooner.

Ye gods! Just tell me, man!

But the prospect is getting clues to the answer now. They're also getting confirmation that the author has qualifications in the subject. He's done it. He's a full-time writer, earning a living from indie publishing.

I want you to have your own March 2.

This is a reinforcement of an emotional trigger point for many artists. They want to earn a living doing what they love. And they'd love to quit the soul-crushing job they're (probably) currently chained to.

And that's what this book is about. I'm passing on, without holding anything back, what I've learned.

Like the Energizer Bunny, this open loop just keeps on giving.

This is not a beginner's book. If you're looking for an introduction to indie publishing, I recommend starting with something like David Gaughran's *Let's Get Digital.*

A statement of fact. The book isn't for beginners. But instead of trying to convince anybody and everybody to buy it, it's referring some of them to the competition!

This is doing two things. It ramps up the scarcity concept. The book is advanced. *And it's dampening down reactance. It's reaffirming the prospect has freedom of choice. No one's trying to talk them into buying.*

This is a book of advanced strategies and tactics. Even veterans with a large backlist will learn quite a few things that they wouldn't expect. But it's also for those who've published several times without the success they want. Or, perhaps, that highly select group who haven't published yet, but who take this business seriously and are tirelessly preparing to make the best start possible.

For them, I offer this advice. All the hard work in the world isn't enough. That labor must be guided by correct knowledge, or the effort is lost.

Jeepers creepers! The open loop just keeps tugging, pulling and drawing. What is this damn knowledge?

When you finish this book, please tell me if you think I've given you that knowledge.

This is a covert call to action. The way to find the answers is to read the book. It's not worded with the usual imperative command that an overt CTA uses. There's just the subtle assumption of "when" you finish the book.

There you have it. There's more going on in there than I've said. But those are the important parts. I hasten to add that I think the book lives up to the promise of the introduction.

But I *would* say that.

Maps

This is common in epic fantasy. I don't think I've seen it elsewhere.

It's all about the target audience, and many readers in epic fantasy *love* a good map. I'm one of them.

People outside the genre probably don't get it. Some people within the genre don't get it either. You can't please everyone.

If you have a map, the front is a good place to put it. Overall, it's a selling point and a feature of high interest.

But, it all comes down to execution. It all comes down to providing value to your target audience. That's what holds attention and begins to transform interest into desire.

If you have a handsome map, detailed with forests and towns and mountains and roads and all the goodies that readers like, this is great. They may study it for a while before moving toward your opening chapter. They're probably going to start forming opinions of how good your worldbuilding is as an author, and whether your taste in names resonates with their own.

On the other hand, if you have a dull map, with barely any detail, what sort of impression is that giving the prospect?

Whether it's a map, or anything else, always decide if you're feeding into the halo effect or the horns effect. Then add or delete accordingly.

Repeating the blurb

This is more common than you might think. It does serve a purpose. Its origin, I think, is with authors who use permafree. But the practice has spread beyond that.

The idea is that if someone downloads a book for free (or even buys it), they may not read it straightaway. They probably have a hoard of free books stashed away, and it could take weeks or months (if ever) to get to this particular one. But when they do, the blurb gives them a refresher of what type of book it is, and probably reminds them of why they downloaded it in the first place.

Your turn. Halo or horns for this? Does it create a good first impression or a bad one?

This is what I think. Despite serving a purpose (weeks or months after the download) it's a case of horns. As the saying goes, a bird in the hand is worth two in the bush. (I feel sorry for the bird in hand. It's destined for pigeon pie or something. But I digress.)

My first concern as an author would be to secure that initial download. In this respect, the prospect has just read the blurb before they clicked on the preview. Then they get hit with it again? Boring. Possibly even annoying. The horns effect is triggered.

It's certainly true that the prospect will see what it is after a moment, and then scroll past it. It's near effortless to do so. But that slight annoyance lingers, and what if you had a dud table of contents and a boring dedication as well? These things start to add up. A pattern begins to form in the prospect's mind. You want it to be a good one, not a bad one.

Review quotes

As is often the case, there's no right or wrong answer here. You can use them in the frontmatter of a book, or not – just make sure that if you do, the execution is good.

What's a good execution?

I would say no more than three quotes. Sometimes, you'll see a page of them. This is boring to a prospect. No matter how good they all are, no one wants to read them in bulk. The prospect wants your book, not an endless stream of sugary praise.

Pick the best one, or two or three. Make sure they're short. They offer social proof, which is a selling point, but not all social proof is equal.

There's a whole lot of science around social proof, but for our purposes it boils down to this. People are more strongly influenced by people they relate too. This means that the pecking order goes like this:

Other authors in the genre
Readers in the genre
The literary establishment, magazines and blogs

It may have surprised you that the literary establishment is the least influential. But research from BookBub confirms this. It also fits in with the neuroscience better.

Who do you trust more? Whose opinion do you value more highly? Writers and readers, or institutions?

For those interested, I delve more deeply into this in book two of the series which deals with blurbs. That's where review quotes are more commonly found.

A list of your other books

Some prospects may be impressed by your productivity. Especially if the list shows that you've completed a number of books in the series after the one that they've clicked on.

But I have to ask again, halo or horns? What's going to do the best job of selling the book they're interested in right now? A list of other books, or chapter one of the story they've just clicked on?

For myself, I'm reminded of a Bruce Lee Quote. *Absorb what is useful. Reject what is useless.*

You decide, grasshopper. What's going to serve you best?

Better still. What's going to serve your *prospect* best?

A cast of characters

Some people like to get fancy and label this a dramatis personae. Maybe it's just an epic fantasy thing, or maybe it's more widespread than that.

But if you include such a list in your frontmatter, this is my question to you. Is it a selling point?

If you answer yes, let me ask you another. Is it a better selling point than your first chapter?

If you answer yes to that, may I humbly suggest your first chapter needs a rewrite?

Nuff said, as the great writers would eloquently put it.

I'm not going to harp on. You get the drift now. The question, as always, is whether or not including something is going to heighten the halo effect, or produce the horns effect. More succinctly, omit what reduces the chances of a sale and include what increases it.

This may surprise you, but an about the author section or an author biography is an incredibly valuable sales tool. It's an opportunity missed by most authors.

If that's you, you can rectify that. I'll show you how in an upcoming chapter. But does it belong in the frontmatter? I've seen it there in nonfiction and fiction alike.

In nonfiction, probably it does belong there. Especially if it shows your qualifications on the subject at hand. But not in fiction. There, it's just getting in the way of the story the prospect wants to read.

Is this ever a good thing?

5. The Art of Nonfiction Blurbs

There are some who say there's not much difference between a fiction and a nonfiction blurb.

Have you ever seen *How to Lose A Guy in 10 Days*? I'm certainly not as cute as Kate Hudson, nor even as cute as Matthew McConaughey, but just like Ms. Hudson in the card-game scene – I call BS.

Indie publishing is a burgeoning industry, flush with growth, ripe with potential, and a target for con artists, insta-experts and fast-buck hustlers.

Misinformation is rife, mostly spread by people pretending to have knowledge they don't possess. Because they have a book to sell in an underserved niche, or an expensive course to sell to the unsuspecting. And after that, a secret Facebook group to wring more money out of their targets.

Don't get me wrong. There's a lot of good information out there too. And books and courses. Just choose wisely.

Nonfiction blurbs are standard sales copy. The book is a product, and the sales copy an ad. It's that simple.

But not all sales copy is the same. There are different approaches. There are many, many copywriting formulas. For nonfiction, I personally favor identify, agitate and solve. But here's another good one:

Before – this is your world…
After – imagine solving this problem
Bridge – here's how to get there

The two formulas are fairly similar. Depending on your book, you might choose one over the other.

Fiction blurbs are different. In truth, fiction is a product the same as, say, cherry Chapstick. Except the product is really something else at the same time. In this case, art.

Fiction blurbs are unique in the copywriting world, except for maybe movie trailers. They bring copywriting and art together into a fusion. A fiction blurb is an extension of the story itself, usually told from the point of view of a character in the book. No matter how you tweak it, it's not your standard ad for cherry Chapstick.

If you're interested in fiction blurbs, book two in this series is on that subject.

So, let's turn to nonfiction. How should you write it? First, know your audience. What problems and difficulties do they face? What books or sources of information already exist to solve their problems? Are these sources good? How is your book different? How will it help them? What help do they need?

Once you know your audience, then choose your copywriting formula. You know my top pick for this particular job. Identify, agitate and solve. And overlaid with a touch of the AIDA formula, too. Especially the opening hook.

Once again, I'll use some of my own copy as an example. I'll break it up, adding my comments in italics. This is the blurb for my book on, well, fiction blurbs:

Do you sell as many books as you want to?

The tagline stands by itself and is bolded to draw the eye. The prospect is addressed directly, twice, with the word you. You is a power word in sales copy. It's not as personal as using someone's name, but it's more personal than talking about people in general.

A personal approach focuses the prospect's thoughts and responses. This is about them.

The tagline also poses a direct question. Again, this focuses the prospect's attention. When asked a question, a person's mind immediately engages to try to answer it. It's how humans are wired, and copywriters love it.

The subject matter is also clearly signaled. This is a book on how to sell more books. That's a high interest subject to every author. They know the rest of the blurb is going to be about answering the posed question.

In short, the tagline attracts attention, and focuses it on a problem the prospect likely wants fixed.

A blurb is the hub around which all buying decisions revolve. People click to it from the cover. They click to it from ads. They click to it from other books. But how do you write one that turns views into sales?

This narrows the focus. It identifies blurbs as a key element of the problem. They're central to selling books, but writing ones that convert impressions into sales is a part of publishing that most authors struggle with. And again, the prospect is engaged with a direct question and a "you".

Do you get conflicting advice on how to write a blurb from books, blog posts and internet comments? Have you tried gimmicks from blurb gurus only to see no difference in sales?

Agitating the problem. Continuing with direct questions and the use of "you".

This book delivers methods that will work for you. It studies blurbs from a copywriting, neuroscience and artistic perspective.

Because a good blurb is all these things.

A confident statement that a solution exists. And a hint of what that solution is.

This book will dispel blurb myths, and explain effective tactics. Finally, it'll deconstruct great blurbs so you see their moving parts.

More foreshadowing of the solution. And a promise of a detailed and comprehensive treatment.

Enter the cutting-edge world of advanced blurbs and learn:

Cutting-edge and advanced serve to create scarcity. This is no ordinary run-of-the-mill book on blurbs.

The blurb then breaks off into dot points.

The neuroscience behind persuasion

This is a good dot point to introduce some actual neuroscience. The neuroscience of persuasion is well-known in behavioral economics circles, but it's catching on in marketing as well.

Words are information. Words are data processed by the brain, in a way similar to incoming data about whether it's hot or cold, whether the sabre-tooth tiger is moving closer or moving away, or whether food tastes good to eat or bad. All the body's senses are transmitting huge volumes of data to the brain every minute, and the brain interprets that data and sends signals back to the body on how to respond. For instance, if it's cold, the response might be to shiver in order to generate heat.

By far, the majority of these responses are unconscious. One of these responses is triggered by novelty. By new information that hasn't been processed before.

Authors are familiar with some elements of marketing, but this dot point takes it in a direction they've never seen before. The neuroscience of persuasion. That's a novelty. It's new. It deserves extra attention so the brain can figure out how to deal with it.

The brain's response to novel situations? It happens in a region called the ventral striatum, which is directly connected to the amygdala. Novelty excites this part of the brain, which causes a release of dopamine. The dopamine (which makes us feel good) also motivates us to take action. It's the brain's way of nudging us to explore and obtain more data.

Let me simplify that. Novelty excites us, and makes us feel good. It encourages us to explore. This is a powerful response in sales copy. This is the perfect mindset to encourage someone to buy.

We'll return to this concept a few more times in the chapters to come. As the dot point says, it's at the cutting edge of persuasion. And marketing.

The bad advice that's killing your sales

Killing is a strong word. It's an emotional word. This dot point continues to agitate the problem.

Copywriting super-hooks other than teasers

What's a super-hook? Are there really hooks other than teasers? These are open loops.

How blurbs *really* work

A promise of information to come, which invokes anticipation.

Distilled here is decades of knowledge from a fulltime author who used to be employed to persuade people.

The author isn't an insta-expert. He used to do this for a living, and was paid to do so by other people. This is social proof.

You'll never look at blurbs the same way again. Are you ready to unleash the full power of yours? You can start now.

This is reaffirming the novelty aspect. There's information here not presented in any other book on blurbs. It also nudges the prospect's emotions with words such as "unleash" and "power". They give a motivational vibe to the copy, and a sense of what can be achieved.

This is followed by the soft CTA of "You can start now." Again, this addresses the prospect directly, and reminds them that they can take direct and immediate action. That action, of course, is to buy the book. But it's not a hard sell. The soft CTA acknowledges they have complete freedom of choice and therefore avoids reactance. A hard sell would have been something like "Start now!". And that likely would cause reactance, at least in a book blurb where CTAs aren't traditionally used.

There you go. That's my take on the art, and also the science, of writing a nonfiction blurb. There's a crossover of techniques between fiction and nonfiction, but they're not the same thing at all. Nowhere near it. And if someone says otherwise (possibly because they have a book on fiction blurbs but don't want to lose a paying customer looking for advice on nonfiction), just picture Kate Hudson calling BS.

6. Author Biographies Unleashed

Author biographies contribute to sales. Not as much as blurbs or even covers, but they help to sell books.

How?

Amazon is often a black box, giving us nothing about how they operate or how prospects browse the digital store.

But they don't really have to. Like any professional website, the setup of the Kindle Store reflects customer behavior. The things clients can see are there because Amazon knows they want to see them. The order of their appearance signifies a hierarchy of customer priorities.

If you had the time and money, that's how you'd set up the store too, yes? Show the customer what they want to see, and in the order they want to see it.

Using this mindset, what can we say about the author biography section?

First, on every product page the author's name appears in the top left corner along with other critical bits of information such as price, review numbers and the average review rating. More than that, the author's name is a clickable link.

Amazon wouldn't make it a link if a reasonable percentage of people didn't click on it to check out the author. What that percentage is, only Amazon knows. But if it were insignificant, they'd remove the link and keep people on the product page.

Clicking the link, we're taken to a new page. At the top left is the author biography, with a "follow" button. The follow button is important, as readers are more trusting of "following" an author on Amazon than of giving their email addresses away to a private subscriber list that might spam them.

And, critically, all this is on the top left of the page. This is the most important, and most seen, part of any webpage. It gets more eyeballs on it than anywhere else. Google "heatmap of webpage" or "F-shaped scanning pattern" and look at the images for verification.

We're not done yet. The biography is *also* on the product page that we left just a moment ago. Here, it shows below the blurb but above the reviews. In short, Amazon is willing to take up critical space on their webpages to show your biography. Twice. And each time in an important place.

So, we've established that the biography is important to prospects, and that it serves a critical purpose of collecting "followers" that Amazon will notify when you release a new book, thereby garnering you sales and momentum in the store. But what should the biography say? And how should it say it?

You really have to look at this in two different ways, because there are two different types of prospect looking at your biography. Those who have bought one of your books before, and those who haven't.

This makes your job a bit harder, because you still only get one biography and one choice of wording for all to see.

But it depends on what action you want the prospect to take after reading. And there are multiple options.

The thing to remember is that any point of contact you have with a prospect, whether on a product page or elsewhere, is a point of contact where the prospect evaluates you. Do they like you? Or not. Do they like your writing style? Or not. Do you engage them? Or not. Are they more likely to buy, follow you, visit your website or sign up to your mailing list? Or not.

Do you see now why your biography is sales copy? Do you see value in deciding what you want it to achieve, and choosing the wording that fulfills that purpose?

Fortunately, you can do a few things at once here. The most important of all is to engage the prospect. The biography should entertain, and generally it should do so in a way that reflects the style of your books. It's a way for the prospect to decide if they like your writing style.

Giving a dry list of facts, because that's what you saw someone else do (who isn't a copywriter) doesn't engage.

The author was born in Seattle in in 1974. As they grew up, they developed an interest in the history of the American West. After…

Boring. No one really wants to read a list of facts and figures. The biography should not be about that sort of stuff. It should be about what the author *thinks* and *feels*. That's a true biography, not what year they happen to have been born in.

Thinks and feels. This is taking us into the realm of emotions again. Embrace this, and it'll serve you well. That's what people are interested in. Emotional connection.

And what sparks an emotional connection? The first place to start is authenticity. If you write your blurb in third person, do you really think you're fooling your audience?

I don't think so. They know you're an indie author. They know that no publisher or marketing department wrote your biography.

My suggestion is to embrace who and what you are. This is being authentic. It's being genuine.

It's a theme of this book that many of the old ways of marketing are outdated. They don't work like they used to. People are wide-awake to marketing tactics. The remedy for that is not to come up with better tactics … it's to be authentic.

Tactics trigger reactance. Authenticity triggers engagement.

Still on the fence about this? I suggest a Google search such as "The value of authenticity in marketing". It'll blow your mind.

Old-school push-marketing is dying. So many places you go in the indie-author world, you're getting taught outdated and ineffective approaches by people who have no background in business, marketing or persuasion. But if you widen your horizons and question the self-proclaimed gurus, you'll enter a new world full of promise. Not snake oil.

Back to third person. The above was a long-winded way of saying first person is authentic. It's genuine. It's engaging. It's the real you, not a smokescreen of marketing. Third person is disingenuous. Do you really want to start a relationship with the prospect based on a lie? Even if it's a white lie.

This is not what you've been told. You've been told your biography should be third person. That's professional.

What do I say?

I call BS again. There's a massive movement now in marketing circles toward first-person advertising. It brings you closer to your audience. It doesn't have the feel of an authority talking *at* someone, but of a person talking *to* someone. It's gold. And I recommend it whether someone is an indie *or* a traditionally published author.

Moving along. Regardless of whether the biography is in first or third person, what should it say?

Whatever it says, it should be interesting. It should *not* be a list of facts. It should evoke emotion. Preferably, it should give information about your life that relates to your fiction or nonfiction books.

That last suggestion is easy for nonfiction. If you've written a book on, say, Facebook ads, beer brewing or copywriting, your biography should give information about how you acquired your expertise. Duh. But note, you should actually possess said expertise. Not possessing it makes you a pretender, and you'll probably want to omit any reference to it in your biography.

Fiction is somewhat harder. If you write comedy, your biography should reflect that. If you write military thrillers, I would certainly mention any military background. This isn't necessary though. For instance, I'm pretty sure most spy novelists aren't really spies. Any more than Roger Moore worked for MI6. Then again, you just never know. Spies are usually the people you least expect.

Whatever the type of story, try to make your biography resonate with the genre, one way or the other.

Time to discuss structure. AIDA is the formula that applies here. You want to get attention on the first line, and then hold it. You'd better, because on Amazon there's only a snippet of biography available above the fold. After that, the prospect has to click to read more.

You want them to do that. You want to engage them. You want to talk to them. You want to build a relationship with them. You want to interest them, and then turn that interest into desire … for something.

The something is up to you. I'm not the Amazon Police, so some of the examples I give below, although common enough, may not be something Amazon really wants you to do. Then again, their rules are vague, so it's hard to know.

However you choose to end the biography, it should be some sort of CTA.

One that you could use is your website address. Check Amazon's rules about this though. All I can find is a prohibition against doing this in a product description. Amazon's Help Pages don't mention anything about websites in author biographies. Nor does Author Central, where your biography is actually uploaded. It's unclear to me what the specific rule is here, so tread carefully. But right next to your biography Amazon allows a link to your blog posts on your website.

Perhaps the difference is that you can give your website address in the biography (which authors often do), but not make it a clickable link, whereas your blog feed is clickable.

At any rate, inform yourself of the rules and make your own decision accordingly. The same applies if you place a link to your subscription service provider, for instance Mailchimp.

The ultimate goal is to obtain signups to your mailing list. These will likely only come from previous readers rather than potential readers.

That leads to the next potential CTA – suggesting the prospect click the "Follow" button on Amazon. This achieves a similar thing as above. It's a safer choice though. On the other hand, Amazon is notorious for unreliability as to when, and sometimes even if, they notify followers of a new release. In addition, you have no way to personally contact such followers.

Another option is to have some sort of soft CTA to buy your books. The problem with this is that the prospects fall into different groups. Those who have never (yet) read any of your books, and those who have read some. And those who have read all of them. This makes for a bad CTA recipe. However you word the CTA, it's going to be ineffective on a significant number of readers. Not to mention, the prospect has probably looked at the biography to find out something about you as a person. Finishing with your website address is more in tune with that. This will give them value, for instance, through blog posts or some sort of resource you have there. And of course, your website will also have a mailing list signup option.

Of course, you may prefer to engage your readers via a Facebook group or Twitter. One highly successful author (H.M. Ward) even offers a text number that you can use to get text reminders for new releases. That's some forward thinking there, and something different that stands out from the crowd. It likely appeals to her target demographic, too.

You could include multiple contact points. Maybe your prospect prefers Twitter to Facebook. Or signing up to a mailing list. But be careful of this. It's okay to give them options, but too many options interfere with decision-making. Too many options can lead to none of them being taken. So, I'd limit this to three. One would probably be even better.

7. Newsletter Sales Copy

This is not a chapter on how to *run* a newsletter subscription list. Or even how to build it.

Choices of how often to email your list, and when, don't strictly speaking fall inside the definition of "sales copy". These are business and marketing decisions.

But I do have an opinion.

I suspect you guessed I would.

All the experts will tell you that you should email your list regularly (perhaps weekly but certainly monthly at a minimum) to keep them warm or engaged.

The experts are probably right. Certainly, this is outside my field of expertise, and they know better.

Then again, it's dangerous to think like that. Are they *really* experts? If what I see passing as expert advice for authors in respect of copywriting is an example ... some of the advice about newsletters might be questionable, and possibly designed with one purpose in mind – to separate you from your cash. Or given by someone who thinks they're such a genius that they can write a book on a subject despite having no background in it, and that just having read a book or two on the topic qualifies them as experts. I won't even start on their $500 or $1000 courses.

Sorry to be negative. But it irks me that so many people see indies as a way to make a fast buck. This is an industry that attracts con artists like an emotionally broken billionaire bad boy attracts the girls in a romance story.

Enough of that. The only advice I'll give on the topic of running a list is to be authentic. Deliver what people sign up for. If you tell them up front that you'll be emailing regularly, and you'll be informing them of what your dogs ate for breakfast and sending them cute pictures of your cat, well, if they signed up for it go ahead.

On the other hand, if they've signed up because they want to know when you have a new book coming out, give them that. And only that.

There are people who love to engage with authors. They want to talk. They *want* to know what your dog ate for breakfast. I'm not one of them. Jeepers creepers. I can't even remember what *I* ate for breakfast. I hope it was a marzipan brownie though.

Genre and demographics play a role here. If you write romance, and your readers are female, they may love regular engagement. Or not. There's no one size fits all answer here. Just know what you feel comfortable with as an author, and what your audience *wants*. Not what they'll *tolerate*.

For myself, I don't have the time or inclination to email regularly. I email when I have a new release, which is all I promise at the signup stage.

Some of you will have noticed that I don't even *have* a newsletter signup for this book series. That's a deliberate choice. I'm publishing these books in a rapid-release schedule, and then that's it. I don't envision any more. So a subscription list isn't going to do me much good. I'd rather, by far, use the backmatter to point people toward my Facebook group and build a community interested in real copywriting skills and the cutting edge of indie book marketing.

So, to sum up, begin your list as you mean to keep going with it. Don't email weekly if that's not you. Emailing for new releases only is fine. The sky won't fall down. Just work out what suits you, and what suits your audience. And be authentic.

What I'll give now is just a personal opinion. Frankly, I'm over signing up for emails. When I do, I hate getting blitzed by a whole bunch of autoresponder rubbish pretending to be personal and trying to sell me something and lure me in deeper. If you've written a good book though, I want to know when the next one comes out.

But that's just me. Maybe I'm a simpleton. But I know what I like and what I don't.

What I really, really dislike is signing up for an author's new releases only to find that they advertise other authors through their emails. Hot diggity hell no, that annoys me. As if they know my taste in books.

This, of course, is never worded as an ad. It comes across as a personal recommendation. Sometimes this is true, but for the most part it's a newsletter swap or a paid-for promotion.

There's another reason you see these books being "recommended". It goes like this. "A good friend of mine recently released a new book. I think you'll love it. Yada yada yada."

Often, this is just a sneaky tactic. Good friend my pale, white ass. The true motivation is not to help out a so-called friend. The author has spotted a book they think will rise high in the rankings. If they catch things early and make a recommendation, they just might get on it's also-boughts and hitch a ride.

I'll give this tactic a nod for having the smarts.

But is it authentic? You decide.

Are we there yet? Yes we are. Time to talk sales copy.

The sales copy for a newsletter email starts with the subject line.

The first step here is to try to avoid spam triggers. You want to give your email the best chance of showing in the prospect's inbox, and not being filtered away into a spam folder.

There are trigger words for this.

What are they?

They tend to change a bit depending on what's going on in the interweb at any given time, but a good guide is that if it sounds like one of the spam emails you receive, *don't use that wording.*

The best way forward is to periodically do a Google search for "spam triggers 2019" – or whatever year applies. If you're not familiar with the topic, this is crucial. Please look it up.

There are far too many for me to list here, but here are a few samples. Symbols such as $ or % can trigger spam filters. Think spammy emails such as "save $" or "100% satisfaction". Some of the words are: Free. Amazing. Discount. Get. Hello. Offer. Price. The list keeps on going, because there are hundreds.

Right. We've established what not to say in the subject line. Now, what *should* you say?

We're going to call on AIDA here again. You want attention. Just not from the spam filters. The subject line should be a hook. I dealt with hooks in book two of this series, so I'm not going to go over the same ground again. Suffice to say, it could be an open loop, a statement, a fact, a direct question etc. If you haven't read book two, you don't have to. Google "Copywriting hooks". That will tell you what you need to know. Just not with my rapier-like wit, disdain for shady indie advisers and references to marzipan brownies.

Or you can ignore hooks, and just go with branding. This works. Big time. Reason being, opening an email is about trust. Worried about spam? Worried about spyware and viruses? Delete. See a subject line from a remembered and trusted source? Open.

Russell Blake is the master of this. His email subject line is always … err … just Russell Blake.

Genius. I know who he is. I know he talks sense. The email is trusted (and wanted). Click – it's opened. Sometimes the simple things in life are the best.

Next, we come to the body of the email. Again, I advise you to follow the AIDA formula here. But first, decide the one true and best purpose of your email. What are you hoping to achieve? This will give you clear direction, and it'll shape every word you write. If you have multiple purposes, you, my friend, are on a slippery slope. Remember Russell Blake. Simplicity works. Don't get too clever.

This is good advice for any sales copy by the way, wherever it appears. Keep your one true goal in mind all the time, and let it shape every choice of wording you make.

Only you know what your goal is when you email your list. It might be to advise them of a new release. Or it could be to just talk to them and build a relationship. Whatever it is, do that and do it well.

Finish it with a CTA, even if you're just relationship building. You might want them to reply. Or check out your Facebook group, or whatever. This is generally soft, but you have more leeway here than in a blurb, especially if you're selling something. These people have signed onto your list to buy your books. If the purpose of the email was to notify your list of a new release, there's nothing wrong with finishing with something like:

BUY ON AMAZON

Better yet, if you're exclusive to Amazon, make it easy for your list in different countries to purchase:

BUY ON AMAZON (USA)
BUY ON AMAZON (UK)

If you're wide, you can say Amazon, Kobo etc. Of course, make the words a clickable link.

One thing to note, you can't be everything to everybody. I would place your best market on top and work your way down. That way the majority of people will see their link first. And I wouldn't include more than four links. Too many options looks untidy and cluttered. Too many choices means the prospect is less likely to click on any of them.

8. Promo Service Mini Blurbs

These come in all shapes and sizes, so there's no one-size-fits-all approach.

Except, in a way, there is. Obviously, you don't need to write a mini blurb for a site that only uses your cover image and book name. Other sites will write their own mini blurb, or just use your full blurb.

We needn't concern ourselves with those.

But when you do have to write your own sales copy, I suggest approaching it from this angle. What's in it for the subscribers to a promo service?

This is what's in it for them. They're looking for bargains. They're relying on a third-party service to provide them notification of said bargains via email, and they're doing that in preference to the time-consuming job of getting on Amazon themselves and searching for reading material.

These two factors predispose the target audience to snap decisions. Bargain hunting by its nature lends the whole process an impulse buy feel. It doesn't get much more impulsive than 99 cents or free. And that they're using a service instead of looking themselves indicates they're time poor. They're not spending what time they do have trawling through thousands of books on Amazon.

How can you use this psychological profiling in your sales copy? You won't need to mention the price. The promo service will have that on your ad. And it's not a selling point either, because all the books being promoted that day by the promo service will be similarly discounted. All you need to do is hit hard and fast with the copy. Start, right from the first words, to set a hook. Make it short, sweet and strong. Make it genre relevant. Make it something that stands out at a glance, because a glance is all you're likely to get.

Promo service users are likely in a hurry, and likely making snap judgements the way people eat chips when they're bored of waiting in a queue: just one after another.

Don't give them unusual names right up front. Or complex sentences. Or backstory. Treat the mini blurb as a tagline.

That leads to the next point. Keep it short. The promo services that get you to write your own copy have different length requirements. Some of them allow little more space than a tagline, others more. I suggest you use the minimum you can get away with. But however long it is, frontload your best hook. If space permits, end with a good hook too. And keep everything in between targeted to genre tropes. In other words, keep it all simple and obvious so that it can be digested at a glance.

One other thing. Some promo services tell you not to use your actual blurb for this, either in full or cut down.

They're the smart ones. The ones that let you use the blurb, or just copy it themselves, are doing you a disservice.

If a prospect reads your blurb, or your tagline, in the ad and actually clicks through to your book, you want them to get a feel straight away that they're in the right place. Trust is a big factor with internet clicks. People are careful where they click to, and they're wary of scams and the like.

If you earn that click, don't jar the prospect. That might make them click back. The mini-blurb and the real blurb should resonate with the same genre tropes, even the same hook concept as one another, but the wording should on no account be the same.

If someone tells you a joke, and then they tell it again a few seconds later, it's not as funny the second time around. The same thing applies to ads and blurbs. If the prospect gets hooked by something in the ad, and clicks through to the blurb only to find the same thing, the punch of it is gone. Hit them with something fresh and hooky though, and your allurement is not only maintained but intensified.

Put in that extra bit of work and keep your ad copy different (but still in tune with) your blurb. It'll serve you well. And be wary of promo sites that don't warn you not to use the same copy in both places. If they don't, you have to wonder how good other aspects of their marketing are, and how much they care about conversion rates.

9. Amazon Ad Copy

In many ways, everything that was said in the last chapter applies to Amazon ads as well. But not quite.

Amazon browsers, on the whole, are not in so much of a hurry. They're likely to take more time to make a decision, and they're less likely to be so heavily swayed by a bargain price.

The concept of frontloading a hook, finishing with a hook, hitting genre tropes and not using your tagline from the blurb remains the same though.

What's different then, if anything?

High-end advertisers tend to use keywords in Amazon ads. This isn't necessarily an advantage in persuasion, but it *is* potentially an advantage in your ad's relevancy score. If your book's metadata includes the keyword billionaire, and your ad copy includes the word billionaire, and you're targeting a book called *Bad Boy Billionaire Unleashed*, then Amazon's algorithms might consider your ad more relevant and give it a higher relevancy score. This will result in better ad placement at a cheaper cost per click.

Maybe. It's a theory, and one that frankly I haven't seen any proof for. But you *will* see it at play on the top 100 lists on Amazon where the big boys and girls party. For that reason alone, it should be considered and tested when you're trialing different ads with different copy. Ignoring what the most successful authors are doing is just stupid.

Trial it before you discard it. Or it just might work for you. It hasn't for me, but that doesn't mean it won't for you. Just make sure your copy is good whether you slip in keywords or not.

Another thing you'll see (sometimes) in the copy of the big dogs is references to Kindle Unlimited. It's usually something like "Read for free in KU".

Free is most certainly a power word. Some words have more mojo than others. Just like a billionaire bad boy has more mojo than an accountant. Unless you know a *really* good accountant.

Amazon can be testy when it comes to price references in copy though, so be careful. On the other hand, every ad that you see on the platform is manually approved by them, and you see the "free in KU" thing regularly if you look for it. So presumably they're okay with that wording.

Amazon copy is short, so it's good to use power words there. This applies to any copy, but it can be harder to have good hooks in short copy. And a few power words in short copy can really boost it.

You and free are power words. So is new. Remember how a sense of novelty can trigger a release of dopamine and cause a person to act? New is a great word to include in your copy because it initiates this phenomenon.

Other great power words (at least in the Amazon ecosystem) worth trying are box set and complete series. At least if they apply to you. These are selling points to a lot of people.

Warning! This is another good one that I've seen. Frontload it. I mean literally start with "Warning!" See how it attracts the eye at the beginning of a sentence? It's also a novelty. And it's an open loop, too. This tactic has a lot going for it, but obviously only use it if it's suitable for the mood of your copy. A possible use for it could go like this: *Warning! Don't read this book unless you're prepared for sleepless nights ... or to fall in love with ... or ...* insert something genre appropriate to your book.

This is talking directly to the reader. While we're on that subject, please note that this can be a powerful tool.

It makes the copy stand out in an environment where so much copy is third person. But try it and see if it works in your genre.

Another good phrase I've seen at the end of copy is *get your adventure on*. This was an adventure story. You could swap out adventure for something that worked for your genre. This tactic is *much* better as a buy CTA than buy now, or grab your copy today!

10. YouTube Tips

Sales copy can be produced as written words. Or in video format. Basically, every time you communicate with a prospect, in whatever form or medium, it's an opportunity for persuasion.

Keep that thought in mind. We'll return to it in the next chapter. Keep in mind also that good marketing connects a prospect to a product they want. It's not about sales, sales, sales. That's bad marketing, and despite all the pushing and shoving of that outdated approach (or actually because of it) it's ineffective.

Speaking of ineffective, videos are generally futile for promoting fiction. But, I see enormous scope for nonfiction, and I think this is greatly underutilized. YouTube offers massive potential.

The digital revolution, which has disrupted newspaper, magazine and book publishing industries, has shifted audiences, and audience behavior patterns, on an unprecedented scale. The progression from print to screen has driven an explosive demand for video. Within two years it will account for 82% of all internet traffic.

If you have the inclination, that's something to be a part of.

YouTube pioneered this digital video popularity. It now receives in the order of 30 million visitors each day, and the number of hours people spend watching videos is increasing 60% annually. This success has driven the rise of videos elsewhere. For instance, Facebook released *Watch* to American users initially, and now internationally.

Commercial and social use of video is growing exponentially. It appears across our devices – PCs, notebooks, tablets, phones and even wrist watches. The near future will see videos vie for our attention as we walk down the street, if it isn't already. Video will also soon appear on ATM display screens and e-menus in restaurants.

This popularity is consumer driven. The more it's met, the more people *expect* it to be met. The phenomenon is crossing over from social and commercial use into education, and will also soon permeate work environments. Video saturation is fast approaching, and this will present those who wish to engage in that medium a critical difficulty. When a product type is everywhere, only the most relevant and engaging iterations will gain traction.

This can be you, if you want. There are opportunities. For instance, starting up a channel that helps people on your chosen nonfiction topics. This is content driven marketing. To be clear here, I'm not talking about making YouTube ads. I'm talking about a channel that provides real and useful content that solves people's problems. For free.

Think of this as a loss leader, just as in the book industry you may have book one of a series set to 99 cents or permafree.

But to succeed at this, you have to engage your audience. This will only be achieved by first recognizing that the digital revolution has not just provided new delivery options but transformed *expectations*. Clients want *infotainment*. They favor material that entices their senses and that immerses them in an *experience*. They reject being lectured *at,* and they demand being talked *to*.

This is the modern world. This is the world where sales copy can generate reactance very quickly. Modern consumers are fed up with old-school advertising. Be entertaining, and provide genuine value that solves problems, or die content marketing death.

You can't just get on YouTube and keep hinting, or telling people, to buy your books. Help them. Provide a service. Develop trust. Let them know what other products you have. If they want them, they'll buy them. Especially if you've been providing value.

The difficult part is providing value, but not giving all your knowhow away for free. Find the balance between the two, and YouTube has the potential to organically grow your sales on a massive scale.

But how should you actually make videos?

That falls outside the scope of a sales copy book. But here are a few pointers. I suggest you subscribe to the Sunny Lenarduzzi YouTube channel. She has a wealth of information, in video format, on how to make great videos. More than that, on how to use a YouTube channel to gain leads for your business. In this case, nonfiction books. But I don't quite rule out the possibility of doing the same for fiction. It may be possible, but it would take a lot of skill, effort and a touch of luck.

I suggest you also get Sunny's BOSS YouTube Channel Checklist. She really is the golden girl when it comes to this stuff.

And ensure your videos follow the AIDA formula. Or the identify, agitate and solve formula. That will provide a framework for your wordage, and your copy is really no different than writing an introduction to a book or something like that. Only you go into more detail and actually solve problems. Just pick specific topics with specific fixes. This is where videos are different from books. A book may take hours or days to read, while a video will probably last ten minutes or less.

One more tip. In the book business, a cover should resonate with genre, blurb and the preview. Everything works together toward a unified purpose. Well, it's no different with quality videos. The script, visual elements and auditory elements (music, sound effects etc.) should all work together toward your purpose. They each reflect each other. A good way to grasp this, and the power this has, is to study ads on TV.

11. The Forbidden Frontier

What I'm about to say now is wrong.

At least, you've been told it's wrong. And you probably believed it with good reason. If everyone says something, it's likely correct. If all the experts agree, it's even more likely to be correct.

In this case, you're right to believe it, because not only the insta-experts say it, but also the genuine experts.

But if we've discovered anything in this series of books, it's this. You have to keep an open mind. You have to question opinions. Even expert opinions. Especially expert opinions, because they're the ones that hold sway. They're the ones that shape the rest of the indie world, and their opinions have momentum and end up repeated by everybody.

So, I don't expect to change your mind here. Far from it. But can we agree that it's a good idea to question standard practice? I don't think you want to follow any industry practice or any industry adviser blindly. I think you're willing to look at things with an open mind, assess the situation and make your own decision. And that decision may well be to agree with the experts.

I won't say you're wrong.

What industry practice am I talking about?

The final frontier. The one place that's banned to authors and where we don't go to play.

Reviews.

Specifically, commenting on your own reviews left by readers.

Thou shalt not comment on reviews. Reviews are for readers. No good will come of it if you do.

That's pretty much the advice. I'm not going to talk you out of it. I *can't* talk you out of it, because if this is your prior belief, nothing will change it. I know a thing or two about what neuroscience and psychology call priors. Working for a tax agency and charged with the task of persuading people to pay taxes teaches a young grasshopper a thing or two about priors.

But I *will* put forward an alternative theory. One that you're free to dismiss. And you know that's true.

Everywhere else, we're told to engage our readers. Facebook? Engage 'em. BookBub? Engage 'em? YouTube? Engage 'em. Our website? Engage 'em. While they're in the queue waiting for their morning coffee and marzipan brownie? Engage 'em. And try to swipe the brownie while they're distracted.

Okay. One of those isn't true. You don't need to engage readers who comment on your blog posts...

So, what's the origin of the concept that you shouldn't comment on reviews?

It doesn't come from Amazon. Amazon encourages the practice. If you've ever asked them to moderate a review that claims you're unnaturally friendly with your favorite leather jacket, they'll tell you to comment and dispute the nefarious claim.

The prohibition against commenting on reviews comes from authors.

What's the logic behind it?

There *is* good logic behind it. Expressing a view can get you into trouble. It's not hard to say the wrong thing. You can come across as a loser, whether you're responding to criticism, praise or just plain answering a reader's question.

All of that's true.

But why doesn't it apply to Facebook? Or YouTube? Or your website? Is there less chance of saying something stupid in those places?

I don't think so.

Stupid comments have no prejudice. They'll happily show up wherever you put them, the nasty little blighters.

Could it just be that we're in the habit of engaging authors in some places, but not others? Is it just a practice that authors fall into by tradition, like starting the first word of a new chapter without an indentation? There's no real reason for that, by the way. There could just as easily be an indentation. Or a double indentation. Or a Gothic font. It's just the way it's done ... by tradition.

Interesting.

By following the prohibition against commenting on reviews, are we missing an opportunity to engage with not just prospects, but people who read our books? Even fans?

Why are we not doing the one thing that we're advised to do in *every* other sphere?

The fall back answer, again, is that we may say the wrong thing. But again, that can happen on any platform.

I'll make a prediction here. A bold one. The time will come when the right to comment on any social media or retail platform will be monetized, including Amazon reviews. Already, Amazon requires people to spend $50 a year in the store to leave a review. Facebook has boosted posts. This is a growing trend. The big dogs know the value of engagement, and they want a cut of the action.

One day, industry gurus will advise authors to engage readers on Amazon's review platform, and that it's acceptable to pay a fee to do so.

That may not be one day soon. Then again, it might. I wouldn't be betting against it.

If you look closely, you'll see that a few of the big indie authors already comment on reviews. I'm not going to name names. They wouldn't appreciate it because they'll get pilloried in forums. But they *do* comment on reviews. Keep an eye out, and you'll see. More will follow. I may even start to do so myself. It's just difficult to go against the trend.

Still keeping an open mind on all this?

I think most of you are.

Want some sort of verification for what I'm saying?

I know I would.

I suggest you do a Google search. Something like "Engage customers and respond to reviews".

Warning! Doing that search may make you question everything you've ever heard from indie author gurus, even the real ones.

But you know my motto in this series: Dig deep. Find the truth. Question standard practice – seek *best* practice.

Only you can decide what best practice is for you. I'm not trying to convince you one way or the other. Mostly, because I haven't made a final decision yet myself. I'm just suggesting you ask yourself the same question that I'm currently asking myself.

Am I missing a great opportunity here?

For those who do decide to engage their audience via reviews, I offer a few tips. I haven't decided to do it yet, but I *have* given thought to how it should be done – just in case.

There's no need to respond to every review. Choose which ones you respond to, and what you say, carefully. It might be a thank you to a heartfelt review that was incredibly insightful. It might be an answer to a direct question from a reader, for instance, asking when the next book in the series will be released. If a reviewer compares you to another author, perhaps you might reveal that you were influenced by that author and loved their books.

There's no need to respond to a reviewer who doesn't like your book. They're entitled not to like it. Responding in that situation is just plain stupid.

But what if the reviewer is factually wrong? You can politely and professionally point out the error. Do it in a way that enables them to save face. Or maybe if it's an obvious error on their part, you can ignore it. Other readers will see their mistake and it won't impact your sales.

But make no mistake. Reviews influence sales. Big time. If a review is plain wrong, but not obviously wrong to readers, it will cost you sales. For instance, an American reviewer commenting on your bad spelling … when the book is written in British English. Or a reviewer of historical fiction who says you've got important dates wrong, when you haven't.

But really, responding to reviews isn't about the negative side. It's about engaging your audience. It's about developing a relationship with the people who read and like your books. That's the untapped reservoir of potential that exists.

So, I ask again. Are we missing an opportunity here? Are we passing up a chance to be ahead of the marketing curve, for once?

Tentatively, I say yes. And I urge you to do the Google search I mentioned above, if you haven't already. "Engage customers and respond to reviews".

If we're missing a trick here, it might just be time to fix it.

12. BookBub Sales Copy

As always, you have to adapt your sales copy to the target audience and the platform on which it's delivered. BookBub ads are no different.

BookBub readers want discounted books. They're accustomed to discounted books. They *expect* discounted books. For this reason, I've never found it an advantage to include the price. This is always 99 cents. I only ever advertise a temporarily, but heavily discounted, book there.

I mention this for a reason. Text space on a BookBub ad is extremely limited. Use only what you need and nothing else.

Actually, that's the key to BookBub ads. Keep them simple.

Let's start with the image. You can use the automatic background that BookBub provides. It works better sometimes than other times. Overall, it doesn't give the best results. But it's not useless either.

Personally, I create my own design and keep it super simple. This is by necessity, since I have zero design talent. I just use black. Jet black. This is easy to produce, but it stands out in an ad, mostly because no one else uses it. Ever. At least that I've seen. And it also allows a great contrast to whatever goes on the foreground.

Standing out is essential here, because your ad comes at the bottom of the featured deals. This makes your ad statistically less seen than what comes before it. Your first job, therefore, is to draw the eye.

I use an image of an ebook cover. I do *not* use a 3D image of a paperback. I trialed this and results were not as good as the Kindle cover.

That might just be me. You always have to trial things for yourself and your own books. But the paperback book sends a message of paperbacks. And people aren't buying paperbacks from BookBub emails.

For the text, I use goldenrod. Gold on black sends a signal of quality. For those unaware, the psychology of color marketing is a thing. It makes a difference. Sometimes a big difference. If you're not familiar with this, I recommend you research it.

The wording I use goes like this, although I vary it.

LOVE
TOLKIEN,
BROOKS AND EDDINGS?

TRY

ROBERT RYAN.

A few things to note. The text is only eight words. Even so, it's probably too much for a BookBub ad. I would certainly never use more. You're looking for a simple message that's easy to read in just a glance.

The idea is to work with what you've got. Embrace the shortness of text in a BookBub ad. Don't try to fight it and cram more words in. *More* words don't sell. The *right* words do.

The wording is based on the "If you like X, you'll like Y" formula. However, you'll notice I don't actually say "you'll like".

Want to guess why?

You've got it, grasshopper. Reactance.

The first reaction people have to being told that they'll like something is to push back against it. Being told they *will* like it is taking away their choices. This is trying to herd cattle again. The wrong way. The "You'll like this because" type formula is subpar copywriting that even most hacks shun.

"Try" is short and sweet. It's suggestive of novelty again, which as you now know stimulates the release of dopamine and encourages people to take action. But it doesn't try to force them. The choice remains theirs.

Why does the comparison formula work?

BookBub buyers are in a hurry. They're looking for discounted books, and they make fast choices. *Discounting price also reduces time spent deciding.* The comparison formula plays right into this. It tells them what they want to know, and it does it fast. In my case, Tolkien, Brooks and Eddings are really well known. They also wrote classic epic fantasy, which is what I write. If I wrote Grimdark, I'd use George R.R. Martin. Keep in mind, I don't compare myself to these great authors. That would be a numbskull move. I merely suggest that if they like them, they might want to "try" me.

For British BookBub ads, I use the same ad, but I swap out Eddings and insert Gemmell. David Gemmell is loved in Britain.

As always in copywriting, know your audience.

These ads, by the way, garner me about a 3% click through, which is pretty good for BookBub ads. When I target well, click through exceeds 7%.

I've mentioned this before, but it can bear repeating. Don't use the tagline of your blurb. Come up with new creative for ads.

Let's circle back to the comparison formula and look at it from a neuroscience perspective. It's not an open loop. It's not a teaser. It's a hook of the statement kind.

It's a hook that tells people exactly what to expect, and there's no aura of mystique or intrigue about it. At all.

But it works. And it works very well.

Why?

Because it's tapping into the anticipation effect described earlier in this book. Anticipation of a known thing can be more powerful than the curiosity of an open loop. When the brain anticipates a positive event, dopamine is released. This makes people feel good, and it encourages them to act.

If you want someone to do something, make them feel good about it.

If you want them to take no action? Fear is a better motivator here. Fear causes different hormones to circulate through the body. People freeze, or even actively disengage. They don't want to act. This is one of the reasons why, in my former role as a government persuader trying to get people to pay outstanding tax, the threat of fines and penalties was ineffective. Positive associations nudge people toward taking action, but negative associations nudge them toward inaction.

What does all this prove? It shows that the psychology of persuasion is far more complex than just using open loops. The concept that ads (or taglines) need open loops to be effective is amateur copywriting. True sales copy, despite its seeming simplicity, is one of the most complex crafts a self-publisher will ever tackle. It pays to delve into it though, because each layer you learn lifts you above your competition.

Let's add another layer now. People love rewards. And sure, in certain sales copy you can provide that. For instance, the offer of a free book in exchange for signing up to a mailing list.

What a reward does is activate a part of the brain called the ventral striatum, and this triggers a release of dopamine. So, a reward does this, even as simple a reward as getting a like on a Facebook comment. Now you know why you crave that little thumbs up so much. (Google "Facebook likes release dopamine" for research.)

We also know that coming across a novelty does the same thing. Finding something new is a kind of reward, or at least processed by the brain in a similar way. I'll speculate that people who like to travel and see new places and have new adventures are addicted to the dopamine hit this gives them. I don't mean this in a bad way. I like a holiday somewhere new as much as anyone.

But this next bit is fascinating. People like to have a choice. This is the opposite state of reactance. Having a choice, like rewards and novelty, also activates the brain's reward system. *Neuroscience shows that our brain perceives choice as a reward.*

Read that again. This is one of the reasons why imprisonment, where basic life choices are dictated by other people, is such a punishment.

Choice also provides a sense of control, which reduces fear and anxiety. Fear and anxiety are the enemy of clicking a buy or subscribe button.

All this is affirmation of why the soft sell of CTAs such as "try" are more effective than the hard sell of "grab your copy now!"

We'll return to the concept of offering a choice in a CTA, specifically when asking for people to join your subscriber list, in the next chapter.

13. Backmatter: Secrets of Success

The backmatter of a book is nearly as important as the blurb the prospect sees at the beginning of the whole process.

Actually, when you think about it, the backmatter isn't so much the end of one book as the beginning of the next. The next book in the series. The next series from the author. Or their entire backlist, if they have one.

Some people will, in fact, list their entire backlist here. I think this is a mistake.

Whether the backlist is one or two books, or dozens, listing them all out looks like a shopping list. And I don't know about you, but I find shopping lists pretty boring. Unless it starts with donuts and ends with brownies.

There's another factor. The more choices you give someone, the harder it is for them to choose. Choices create doubt and uncertainty. At least if there are too many. Doubt and uncertainty kill sales just as quickly as seeing a cockroach crawling over a donut kills your appetite.

Sorry for that imagery. But I wanted to make a point. One of the secrets of backmatter is to reduce it down to the bare essentials. Distill it like a fine whiskey. Make it potent.

A shopping list of books is boring. Unless you're placing mini blurbs with them. But even that will soon get boring. Not to mention drag on for several pages.

My advice is to pick the next most likely book the prospect will want to read, and place a link for it there in your backmatter. The next most likely book is the next one in the series. Or maybe book one of your most popular previous series.

If you have a large backlist, and you don't really write in a series, try this. Put a link there to your author page on Amazon (or other retailers if you're wide). At least that way, the prospect can see your entire backlist – but on a product page where the can actually buy with a click. And your backlist will look good there with your covers and reviews.

But whether you're linking to a single book or your author page, make it a teaser. This little paragraph is as much sales copy as your blurb. It *is* a blurb. Make it enticing. Use hooks. Propel your prospect forward again. They *were* a reader while they read the last book. Now, they're a prospect again. There's no guarantee they'll read more of your books.

But they're warm prospects. Hot even. They're not cold strangers. You have everything going for you here, so don't waste the opportunity.

And as with your new release emails, put in links for your top four stores. Entice the prospect forward, and then make it easy for them to act.

Your backmatter covers a lot of ground. This is all the more reason to keep it as succinct as possible. I'm assuming your highest priority is to sell the next book, so that's why that came first. But you will also want to entice prospects to join your mailing list. Or you may want them to leave a review.

Whichever of these options is most important to you should go first. You have more reader attention just after finishing the story than you do as the backmatter progresses.

Moving along now to your request for people to join your mailing list. As always, you have to ask this: what's in it for them?

If the answer is a free book, well, that's giving them something. If you do have a free book, this sure is the place to pimp it out.

But what if you don't have a free book? Lots and lots of authors don't do free. I'm one of them. How can we still persuade readers to join our mailing lists?

This is hard. This is very hard. It requires top-notch copywriting.

Unfortunately, the standard advice you're given is *not* top-notch.

Does this sound like the familiar spiel?

Visit my website at XYZ and register for my newsletter to keep up to date with new releases.

Or this:

Sign up to my newsletter, and I'll let you know when I have a new release. You'll also be the first to hear about upcoming discounts.

Those are the standard wordings. And here's a secret. Despite my background, when I published my first book, I used something very much like them. Publishing for the first time is time-consuming and a bit daunting. I just followed the lead of what was recommended.

Big mistake.

My first book took off, but I wasn't getting many sign-ups. When I revisited my backmatter, I knew why.

The call to action was bad. The standard call to action, that I'm willing to bet 99.9% of authors use, is not good copywriting.

I cursed myself for a fool, and then I fixed it.

The first thing to ask yourself when you ask someone to do something is this. What's in it for them? Because, you can be sure, they'll be asking themselves that same question.

The answer better be good, or else you're no chance of getting what you want.

A free book offers something. Potentially, it offers something quite good. They might actually enjoy the book, and they'll certainly save themselves a few bucks. This is why the strategy works so well.

Keep in mind that offering a free book to someone who's never read you before is *not* the same as offering one to someone who has. In the second situation, they've already read your writing and they're willing to come back for more. They're fans. Thus, to word it pompously, these people are your people. Only a very small percentage of the first group will turn out to be so.

Enough of free. It works in this situation, but the decision of whether or not to offer free books is far more complex than just your mailing list.

What if you don't offer free? What's the best copy to use?

Not quite so fast, grasshopper.

I haven't done this myself (yet) but there are other tangible enticements you can offer to joining up a mailing list. For instance, in epic fantasy, a fancy-schmancy map would be an inducement. Perhaps in a cookbook it might be a to-die-for recipe (I'd sign up to a mailing list for a marzipan brownie recipe). There are lots of possibilities at play here. Just pick something genre relevant.

The above won't work as well as a free book. But it'll work better than persuasive copy alone.

But now, to the persuasive copy itself. This is what I currently use. I'm not a data guy. I didn't keep statistics of what my sign-up rate was before the change and then after it. My recollection is that it doubled sign-ups. If I ever changed it again, you can be sure I'd keep the exact statistics. But really, what matters is how it might work for you. I suggest you do keep statistics, and trial something like this to see if it works:

Amazon lists millions of titles, and I'm glad you discovered this one. But if you'd like to know when I release a new book, instead of leaving it to chance, sign up for my newsletter. I'll send you an email on publication.

Yes please – Sign me up!

No thanks – I'll take my chances.

Sign me up is, of course, hyperlinked.

So, why did this copy work so well for me? First up, you can see that it uses the identify, agitate and solve formula.

The problem identified is that there's a tsunami of books on Amazon, and finding books you like is difficult. If a book that you want to read is released, how are you going to know about it.

This is a very simple problem. It's a legitimate problem though. Most importantly, it's one that resonates with the prospect. Most of us feel cheated when we discover a new book by an author we like a month or two after it's come out. If we knew, we'd have bought it straightaway and dived into it immediately.

The copy then agitates this problem. The word "discovered" indicates that it's not easy to find books you like. "Leaving it to chance…" continues to agitate.

Toward the end, we move on to the solution. I'll send them an email when I have a new release.

Like all good copy, this is simple. Deceptively simple. But there's more going on than meets the eye.

Two options are given at the end. To sign up, or not to sign up. This doesn't try to trap the prospect. It doesn't try to herd them. And for those reasons, it doesn't trigger reactance.

It's also written from their perspective, not mine. Yes please – Sign *me* up. And No thanks – *I'll* take *my* chances. This is really putting the choice upfront in their mind, and from within, so to speak. And of course, the word "chances" is echoed again, reinforcing the problem and driving home the truth. If they don't sign up, it's only a matter of luck if and when they discover a new release by me.

Sign me up! That's a pretty positive way of wording it. It's enthusiastic. It engenders a feeling of anticipation of good things to come. So we have four things going on here in just the CTA alone. One is positivity. Two is a reward – they'll find out as soon as a new book is released. Third is freedom of choice. Fourth is anticipation of something new.

If you cast your mind back a little ways, you'll see these are things that trigger a dopamine release in the brain, all combined into a single CTA.

I'm actually pretty proud of it.

My CTA has one more thing going for it. It's unusual. I'm willing to bet you've never seen it before (unless you read my fiction as well). If something is unusual, it stands out. It's a novelty. People focus on it.

If this book happens to sell in any significant way, then probably my copy requesting sign-ups will lose that advantage. It'll start popping up in a lot of places. But that's okay. It still has the other advantages going for it.

If you do swipe that wording, I suggest you keep the exact before and after statistics that I never did, and tell me how it worked for you. I'd be interested to see if there's a genre divide on that copy, or if it has a fairly universal effect.

Time to return to the last thing most backmatter contains – a request for a review. That gets a chapter all to itself. In fact, it gets two chapters, because there are two entirely separate ways to look at the issue.

14. The Right Way to Ask for Reviews

Reviews matter. They're important. For this reason, many authors ask for them. They follow the sage advice of "if you don't ask, you don't get."

I'm not going to argue with that sentiment. Largely, it's true.

This is also true. It's a bit of copywriting advice, and you've heard it before in this book. "What's in it for me?"

That's what the prospect will ask themselves when they read your request. And you sure better give them a good reason, otherwise, no matter how much they liked your book, they're not likely to leave a review.

Once again, I'm not a data guy. But I think the review rate when I started publishing back in 2013 (does that qualify me as an indie veteran now?) was about one in a hundred purchases. Now, it's more like one in a thousand.

The times are a-changin'. Or, more accurately, consumer review patterns are changing. Once upon a time, leaving a review was a bit of a novelty. Now, people are browned off. Everywhere they go, whatever book they read, someone is asking for a review. And offering nothing in exchange.

That last part is probably just as well. Incentivizing reviews is the sort of thing that Amazon can ban you for. You know how those stories go. Don't take the chance.

So, how then can you try to up your review rate from nothing to a muscular fly's eyebrow?

Not easily.

But there are a few copywriting and neuroscience methods to try. I'll show you what I do for nonfiction, although the jury is out on how well it works because this series is rapid release and I don't do it for fiction. More on that in the next chapter.

Honestly, I've hesitated to break down the wording of my own review request. It could backfire on me. It could dry up reviews like a parched desert dries up a trickle of water.

On the other hand, I've said elsewhere in this series that my purpose is to hold *nothing* back. And I think you'll appreciate my honesty and transparency. So, this is what I do. This is my review request from my previous book on Amazon ads. My wording is in normal text, and the breakdown in italics.

Here we are. At the end.

I've talked a lot about business in this book. It is, after all, a marketing book. I've used terms like "prospect" instead of "reader". But don't be misled. I'm an artist. I love nothing more than to paint a picture with words. I think there's no nobler art than that of the storyteller.

This is tapping into an emotional psyche. Sure, the book was about marketing, but it's clear that I'm passionate about writing. I love it. My audience loves it. This is a rich vein of emotion, and if you cast your mind back to earlier in this book, I showed how emotions welled up from deep parts of our brain called the amygdalae.

Emotions keep us alive and help us make decisions. Negative emotions like fear generally cause us to take no action or to flee. Positive emotions nudge us to take actions that benefit us. Sadly, people who have suffered injury to these emotion areas of the brain are proof of the idea that decision-making is also rooted in them. They struggle to make any sort of decision at all, even basic day-to-day ordinary stuff. Emotions are critical to decision-making.

Positive emotions trigger a release of dopamine. The dopamine nudges us to act. So, by starting off on an emotional base, I'm predisposing the reader to act. And the act this copy is leading to is to leave a review. You can look at this like turning on the ignition of a car. Doing so is not quite driving, but it's the foundation step to pulling out of your driveway.

What's important to remember here is that while emotions fuel sales copy, they have to be authentic. I really do love writing. If you try to use this technique inauthentically, readers will sense it and reactance will flare to life.

One more thing. I love writing, and my readers love writing. We all love art. This is deepening the sense of rapport between us. A sense of rapport or connectedness is not only emotional of itself, but it's a bond. And people are more likely to do something for a person they identify with than for someone they don't.

But this book will be judged on its merits. It'll be judged by how well it did its job of giving you, the reader, information to help you on your writer's journey.

This is turning people's minds toward a judgement of the book they just read. Was it helpful? Or not. You'll note that nothing is said here to try to sway their opinion. It's just getting them to focus on what their organic opinion is.

Also, the word you is used. Twice. Not to mention your. If you remember, this is a copywriting power word that makes things personal.

What I *hate* after reading a book like this is the feeling that it was stuffed with irrelevant and useless padding. What I *hate* is if the information I paid for was easily available elsewhere on blogs and the like.

This is tapping into emotion again. It's also true. Many books by some indie gurus are nothing more than glorified padding. You'll have read their kind, and doubtless disliked them as much as I do. This is finding common ground between us all. It's bonding again.

If I've done those things to you, I deserve a review bomb. On the other hand, if I've filled each chapter with good information that'll help you run Amazon ads, and I've given you a perspective on things that you haven't seen elsewhere, and most especially, if I've given you correct knowledge that will guide your labor, then I'd like to know that. Tell me in the reviews on Amazon. Tell me if this is a good book. Did I live up to my goal of giving you the information that will enable you to compete with the masses, even *outcompete* them?

This is really making myself vulnerable. It's inviting people to give me a "review bomb" if they thought my book was bad. I wonder how many other authors of guides for indie authors dare do that? I suspect the answer is none.

But this paragraph also emphasizes the two sides of the story. It brings into focus what a bad book does, and then lists what a good book of this kind should do. I've risked the "review bomb" comment because I'm confident that I've put everything I have into these books and that they are, in fact, good. I wouldn't advise anyone to use the "review bomb" comment if they've produced a padded book. Or even worse, pretended expertise in a subject they have no qualifications in just to extract money from authors.

You'll also note that I'm not really asking for a review. Not exactly. I'm talking to them directly with the word you. *And I'm asking them to tell* me *if I've helped them. This is something much more personal, direct and authentic than the standard "reviews help authors find new readers, so please take the time to leave a review."*

Hopefully, if I've built the rapport and bond I've been aiming for in the copy, that request will more likely be answered.

You'll also note that there's no hard sell or coercion going on here. In fact, it's the opposite on an enormous scale. On the one hand, they can give me a review bomb, or a good review on the other. The copy leaves the choice entirely to the reader. Reactance is not triggered.

What the experts say is that I'm supposed to insert a link here to make it easy for you to leave a review. They're not wrong.

Nope. They're not wrong. But readers are bombarded with requests for reviews. I'm doing something different here. Something totally unexpected and novel. This sharpens attention, and by virtue of being novel, it triggers another release of dopamine.

There's another way of looking at this. The human brain is brilliant at observing patterns. Once a pattern is observed, noted and analyzed, it's relegated to the background. This is a survival instinct. The brain can't afford the energy to focus on everything all the time. Once it recognizes a familiar pattern, it ignores it. For instance, walking down a busy street. The give and take, the speeding up and slowing down, the turning and twisting and sidestepping all occur automatically so you don't bump into people. But imagine you suddenly saw a bear ambling toward you. The pattern is broken. *All of a sudden, you're in a new and unprecedented situation. Your mind is suddenly turbo boosted to focus on the bear.*

Doing something totally different in your copy attracts prospect attention in exactly the same way.

But I'm not going to do that. You know how to leave one, if I've helped you.

Neuroscience and behavioral economics have a term for what I've done here. The key to this paragraph is whether or not "I've helped you".

Simple words. A simple concept, but a sophisticated bit of copy.

People much smarter than I am call this reciprocity. Basically, what this means is that if you do something for someone first, they're more likely to reciprocate. So, if I really have helped people with the book, they're more likely to leave the review they know I want. Studies have proven this effect, and it's incredibly valuable.

Another way of looking at this is that's it's a direct answer to the question of "what's in it for me?" The benefit has already been provided, that's all. This is a reminder of it.

The choice, as always, is yours.

This is a final reminder of their total freedom of choice. This is called agency by neuroscientists. It's the antidote to reactance. So, you can see I've used all the triggers for dopamine here. Emotion. Novelty. Freedom of choice (agency). And added reciprocity in to boot.

At the end of the day, you can only ask people to leave a review. Whether they do or not, and whether it's good or not, is entirely up to them. Good copywriting doesn't change that. But it's a lot more helpful than bad copywriting. Or the standard practice and advice churned out in bulk.

Tread your own path, grasshopper.

This has all related to nonfiction. But what about fiction?

Well, you could use the above concepts in fiction. Actually, I suspect it would work really well there. For that matter, in an email too. Even the reciprocity concept could be worked into the copy. I have ideas on how to do that, and I just might write some copy and test it in the backmatter of my next new fiction series. The results won't be in time for this series of nonfiction books, but I'll discuss them in my Facebook group, if you're interested.

15. The Benefits of Not Asking for Reviews

I mentioned earlier that I don't ask for reviews in my fiction books. Maybe I'll change that. I'll probably run a trial with the new series that I've started working on.

But there's a reason I don't.

Actually, once upon a time I did. A long time ago, I ran an experiment between book one of a series under my name, and book one of a series under my pen name.

Both books did well. Both books were priced the same ($2.99 – I've upped my price since then). Both were released close together, and both climbed high on the epic fantasy bestseller list, and ended up selling a near-identical number of copies.

One had a standard request for reviews in the backmatter. One didn't ask reviews at all.

Do you want to know which one got (slightly) more reviews?

You guessed it. The one that *didn't* ask for them.

Now, I know more than I did back then. I've put more thought into the matter of, well, backmatter. I could probably do a better job now. I think I could turn that situation around. It was only one experiment anyway. Although I've since learned from other authors, some of whom sell a lot better than me, that they've found asking for reviews is totally ineffective. (At least from general readers. ARC teams and the like are different.)

But my results did confirm what I already knew in theory.

Reviews are hard to get. Incredibly hard. And to get them above the baseline of those generous people who do it of their own volition, I would have to address the main issue – what's in it for them? That was what the last chapter was chiefly about.

But there are other considerations. There are benefits to *not* asking for reviews.

There are two sides to this. There are prospects who see reviews on Amazon, and who use them as part of their decision-making process of whether or not to buy. And there are those who have already bought your book, and liked it enough to get to the end and see your review request in the backmatter.

In the first scenario, good reviews help the reader to form a good impression. Tick.

In the second, you have to ask yourself what impression your request is giving. The people who see this are far fewer than those who see the reviews, but on the other hand they're far more important. These are your readers. These people paid money to read your book. They are the highest chance of anyone spending more money to read something else you've written.

Which of the two scenarios is the more important relationship?

It's an interesting question. Perhaps, if we accept that both are very important, we don't have to try to squeeze an answer out of our overworked brains.

Both are important. Both make an impression. In all cases, that impression helps shape what the prospect does next.

What impression is given by asking for a review? Here, it doesn't hurt to look at what traditional publishing does. And they do *not* ask for reviews. At least, I've never seen it. Not once in many years of reading.

Perhaps traditional publishing is missing a trick, and indies have the jump on them.

Maybe. It wouldn't be the first time.

The difference though does throw a sharp light on the practice of asking for reviews. You paint a sign on your forehead saying "indie author here" when you do.

I don't think that's a drama. Some authors fool themselves that because they have a good cover, and a well-written book that's neatly formatted, that they're indistinguishable from traditional authors.

I don't believe that for a second. Not a millisecond. I'm even willing to bet my secret stash of marzipan brownies that it isn't true.

Book buyers know an indie author from a traditional author. And if they read indie authors, which judging from the bestseller lists they do as much as, or more than, traditional authors, then they're happy with what they're getting. More than happy.

Distinguishing between the two types of authors isn't a quality thing. There are good books on both sides. And trash on both sides. Distinguishing is a preference thing. What type of story does the prospect like to read? Which authors are giving them that?

But asking for a review brings quality back into it. It does so, because many people see it as unprofessional.

You may not see it as unprofessional. Maybe, in truth, it isn't. Or maybe it is. This is a situation where facts don't help. Not a bit.

The only fact here is what counts to the reader. And it seems that readers, just like writers, are divided on the subject. Some see it as unprofessional. Some aren't bothered. For some it creates an unfavorable impression, for others it slips past them without making an impression at all.

One thing's for sure, for those who don't notice it, or don't care about it, it's still not a selling point. It's either bad or neutral. It's *never* good.

For those who don't like it, the review request comes across as a type of begging. This isn't helped by authors who do, in fact, pretty much beg for reviews. We've all seen requests like this, and lots of them:

I hope you've enjoyed this book. If you have, please take the time to leave an honest review. Reviews help readers find books. They help the author too. The more books I sell, the longer I can continue writing. Your reviews help me to do that.

This is fairly representative. Let's put it through the copywriting filter of "what's in it for me?" The answer, really, is that there's not much in it for the reader. What pressing reason do they have to help other readers find books? What pressing reason do they have to help the author sell books?

The truth is, this is a situation where the only person who gains is the author. They want something. They want something for themselves, and they're asking for it without offering something in return (or at least reminding them of what they've just been given – refer back to reciprocity).

Asking for something without offering something in return? This is getting pretty close to the definition of the word "beg".

Some people respond to beggars, and give them charity. Most people ignore them as though they're invisible.

Either way, it's not seen as professional.

None of this is an attempt to persuade you not to ask for a review, if asking for one is your inclination. It's just an attempt to persuade you to look at the matter from two different sides and to form a well-founded opinion.

Most of all, this is *not* a suggestion to find a way to incentivize reviews. That would certainly produce far better results than just the request by itself, although it would do so at the risk of being banned by Amazon. A risk that far outweighs any potential benefits.

If you do ask for a review, I hope you don't do it by following the standard advice and wording. Think of what's in it for the reader, and try to answer that question, even if it's a retrospective reminder of what they just got.

16. A Master Checklist of Sales Copy

If you've read the previous books in the series, you know that I'm not keen on checklists. They're no substitute for knowing the material you need to know.

But they do have uses. They serve as a memory aid, and they serve to gather some of the key points together in the one place. This better helps you form an overall picture of how a whole bunch of separate items actually work together in unison.

That's never been more the case than it is now. So, here's my checklist of key points from the previous chapters, and a light sprinkle of new ones as a bonus.

But a quick note first. In truth, I felt a temptation to simplify this. I've felt the same temptation with all the books in this series, and every chapter within them. The part of my mind that understands marketing knows the value of a clear and simple message. And here, in a summary, is the opportunity to create a whiz-bang formula with a fancy name that would catch on among the masses. That would require dumbing down the messages, but it would be easy to grasp, and it would sell better. The same with all the books in this series. I could dumb them down. I could give you *Seven Easy Steps to Sizzling Sales Copy*, or the like, and wait for the money to roll in.

But I haven't. There's another part of my mind that has a different aim. It wants to give you the knowledge to succeed. I've read many of the books out there for indie authors, and I've seen what they've done. They've dumbed down and simplified. Worse, some of them were written that way by necessity because the authors themselves didn't know the subject matter.

I refuse to do that. This series of books won't sell as well as it could have because I've chosen to provide the best and the highest level of information that I myself grasp.

I can live with that. Better to sell fewer books, but hold my head high because I gave you the best I had. Even if it is complex.

And it *is* complex. But success requires hard work and determination. It requires thought and an open mind. It will never come from seven easy steps, or the like.

So the decision is yours. Will you give the checklist a quick read and say yup, I've got this? Or will you pick apart this book, and the others in the series, bit by bit and absorb the knowledge until it's second nature?

Righto. I'll get off my soap box now. You know better than I do what information you need, don't need and how to study it.

Time for the checklist, at last. Here it is:

The starting point of any sales copy is a simple question. What's in it for them? "Them" refers to the prospect. If you're thinking of yourself, and of what you can gain, go give yourself an uppercut (or something less violent). Always put the prospect first. Understand what they want. Understand what other people have given them before. Or, to rephrase it into the golden rule of copywriting: know your audience.

Consider the task at hand. What do you want to achieve? Which copywriting formula will serve the situation best? AIDA is the best general formula, bar none. Identify, agitate and solve is a close runner up. But the real best formula is the one that most closely fits the specific task at hand. I've shown my preferences for which formula matches specific situations in the examples in this book. Just remember though, the formulas tend to overlap each other. And they're only a shell. They're a framework around which you build your copy. They're not the copy itself. But they give you direction and purpose without which you'll stumble around in the dark hoping to say something useful.

Strive to find common ground between you and the prospect. The more you want them to challenge their own priors (prior beliefs, attitudes, biases) the more important this is. Some of the points that follow help with this. But ultimately, accept that people have the right to think differently from you. Accept them for who they are, and what they believe.

Build rapport. Build a bond of shared experiences. Help the prospect identify with you. Show that you identify with the prospect. Authenticity is your friend here. Engender a feeling of shared goals and purposes. You have to be genuine to pull this off.

Engage on an emotional level. The deeper and more primitive parts of the brain deal with emotions. And decision-making. And rewards. Most decisions are made at this subconscious level, and then bubble up to the surface. At least the important decisions do. To like something, or not to like it. To want it, or not to want it. To reach out for it, or to shy away from it. Complex problem solving such as $23 + 17 - 14.5 = ?$ engages the uppermost parts of the brain. But this is problem solving. It's not decision-making. Do you see the difference? *Grasp this, and your copy will soar.*

Emotions trigger chemical releases in our brain and the rest of the body. Negative emotions release cortisol. Positive emotions release dopamine. These chemicals predispose us to behave in certain ways.

This is a gross simplification, but cortisol is the fight or flight hormone. This is *not* what you want in your copy. Except when you do. There's evidence that startlement and surprise trigger cortisol and sharpen a person's attention and focus. This is very useful at the beginning of sales copy. For instance, a hook that identifies a problem the prospect experiences. The purpose of said hook is to attract attention. So cortisol isn't the enemy here. But it is at the end of the copy where you want the prospect to take an action.

This is another gross simplification, but dopamine is the feel-good hormone. The more it's released, the more predisposed the prospect is to take an action. Something good will come of it. You especially want to trigger this near the end of your copy and the CTA. But at the beginning of copy is great too. Emotion attracts attention. It gets our interest.

Positive emotions trigger the release of dopamine. So too does getting a reward, receiving information, anticipating information, freedom of choice (agency) and novelty. Integrate these into your copy in order to predispose the prospect toward taking an action at the end.

Reactance is the enemy. The more you overtly try to push someone in a specific direction, the more they resist. This is instinctual. It kills more sales than anything else. This is why the hard sell is the purview of tricksters, con artists and fast-buck hustlers. At least the amateur ones.

Interestingly, this reactance instinct can be incredibly strong and can override rational thought. Some studies show that the horrible and graphic photos depicted on cigarette packages, intended to stop people from smoking, backfire. Some people, after seeing those images, become *less* likely to give up smoking.

Authenticity and freedom of choice are the opposite of reactance. Embrace them, and your copy will flare to life. To do this, keep in mind that good marketing connects a person to a product they want. It does *not* try to convince them to buy.

First impressions count. It's easier for a camel to pass through the eye of a needle than for a bad first impression to turn into a good one. Or something like that. But speaking of religious references, psychologists and marketers deeply study this first impression phenomenon, and how it colors perception afterward. To them, they're known as the halo effect and the horns effect. You want the one and not the other.

Freedom of choice is good. But too many choices swiftly become overwhelming. Never ask for too many things. One CTA is best. After that, results drop quickly. Choose wisely.

Dare to be different. Embrace your authentic self, and let your inner voice flavor your copy. Otherwise, you sound like everyone else. And if you don't stand out, well, you're ordinary. And you'll get ordinary results. Releasing your inner voice can backfire, so it takes courage. If you want to get technical, you can call voice "product differentiation". For authors, our voice *is* our product. You can look at your voice as the most valuable product you possess. When you find it, no one in the world has one just like it.

When appropriate, use reciprocity. It's a powerful tool available to copywriters. To pull it off though, you need a good product. You need to have given the prospect something genuinely good. Fail to do this, and reciprocity won't work for you. It's a two-way street. But this will fall into place if you took step one in this checklist seriously. Know your audience, and ask yourself what's in it for them? If you've answered the question well, reciprocity will be your friend.

Don't be afraid to talk directly to the audience. Ask them direct questions that trigger their mind to try to answer. This engages their attention. It makes them actually consider what you're saying, rather than just scan over it. And of course, use the power word "you".

Just because this book is revealing the cutting edge of copywriting and persuasion, don't neglect the basics. Clear and interesting prose. Good use of whitespace. Open loops. Hooks other than open loops (contrast, statements, facts, startlement etc.) Social proof. Creating scarcity. These will serve you well, too.

Lastly, finish with some sort of CTA. It might be overt, in some situations, especially those that are more obviously advertising such as within an Amazon Sponsored Product ad. But mostly, especially in everyday author tasks, it'll be passive. That is, it won't try to force. It'll provide freedom of choice and not provoke reactance.

There you have it. That's my checklist, but it's just covering the bare bones. For a specific task, please go back to the chapter that deals with it.

17. A Facebook Group to Seek out Best Practice

We've come a long way since the beginning of this book, yes? But all the way through has been the same guiding belief that sparked life into all the previous books of the series: success stems from questioning standard advice and striving for best practice.

Best practice, like Fox Mulder's truth, is out there. But no one person grasps it all. Still less do people share. When they discover a rare truth, they tend to keep it to themselves because it was hard-won knowledge. It's the pretenders who disseminate the most information, the most loudly.

But not always.

There's another way. Sometimes writers *do* share with other writers. I've been fortunate in my career, and I've benefitted from several people like that. I've profited from their generosity. They're one of the reasons I can write for a living.

With this in mind, I've started a Facebook group in that spirit. Its name?

Author Unleashed

Join me there. Our motto is this: Dig deep. Find the truth. Question standard practice – seek *best* practice.

Together, we'll be a group that shares knowledge among ourselves freely. It'll be a place to get feedback on sales copy in all its forms: author biographies, newsletters, backmatter, frontmatter, ads, nonfiction and fiction blurbs. We'll hone them to razor-like effectiveness. It'll be a place to discuss, discover and even drive the cutting edge of marketing for indie authors. Because now you know where that cutting edge is. It's lightyears beyond "start with a hook and finish with a CTA."

Want to be part of that? I look forward to meeting you.

Here we are. At the end.

I've talked a lot about business in this book. It is, after all, a marketing book. I've used terms like "prospect" instead of "reader". But don't be misled. I'm an artist. I love nothing more than to paint a picture with words. I think there's no nobler art than that of the storyteller.

But this book will be judged on its merits. It'll be judged by how well it did its job of giving you, the reader, information to help you on your writer's journey.

What I *hate* after reading a book like this is the feeling that it was stuffed with irrelevant and useless padding. What I *hate* is if the information I paid for was easily available elsewhere on blogs and the like.

If I've done those things to you, I deserve a review bomb.

On the other hand, if I've filled each chapter with good information that'll help you as an indie publisher, and I've given you a perspective on things that you haven't seen elsewhere, and most especially, if I've given you correct knowledge that will guide your labor, then I'd like to know that. Tell me in the reviews on Amazon. Tell me if this is a good book. Did I live up to my goal of giving you professional-level copywriting skills?

What the experts say is that I'm supposed to insert a link here to make it easy for you to leave a review. They're not wrong.

But I'm not going to do that. You know how to leave one, if I've helped you.

The choice, as always, is yours.

Sales copy. Copywriting. Persuasion. Call it what you will, it's a critical step in getting your book in front of readers.

But copywriting only gets eyeballs on your book preview. It doesn't make it sing. It doesn't make your book appeal. It doesn't grip a reader and compel them to turn page after page through the dead of night.

But what if it could?

Preposterous.

Then again, is it so far-fetched that the same behavioral insights that the neuroscience of persuasion brings to copy could help your fiction craft?

Turns out it can. What the great writers of the past did by instinct, neuroscience is starting to explain.

Why do hooks work? Why do we engage with some stories and not others? What characters come to life on a page, and why?

Welcome to the topic of the next book in this series. Like the others, my aim will be to take you places no other indie adviser has taken you before.

Are you up for that?

This knowledge will help you sell more books. It helps *me* sell more books.

I don't have a publishing date for *Bestsellers Unleashed* yet. But, as with this book, I'll leave no stone unturned, and I'll give you that correct knowledge you need. The book will cover topics no other writing guide does, and show you how to write in ways you've never considered.

Interested?

I'll announce the release in my Facebook group if you want to be sure of not missing it.

Thanks for reading. And as always, keep digging for the truth!

Made in the USA
Middletown, DE
14 February 2021

33746276R00066